The Perfect
Audition Monologue

Glenn Alterman

CAREER DEVELOPMENT SERIES

SMITH AND KRAUS

Published by
Smith and Kraus, Inc.
177 Lyme Road, Hanover, NH 03755
www.smithkraus.com

© 2003 by Glenn Alterman

First edition: November 2003
9 8 7 6 5 4 3 2

Cover and text design by Freedom Hill Design, Reading, Vermont

Library of Congress Cataloging-in-Publication Data
Alterman, Glenn, 1946–
The perfect audition monologue / by Glenn Alterman.
p. cm. — (Career development series)
ISBN 1-57525-363-1
1. Monologues. 2. Monologue. 3. Acting—Auditions. 4. American drama—20th century. I. Title. II. Series.

PN2080.A444 2003
792'.028—dc22
2003062534

Contents

APPENDIX A
SAMPLE PLAY SCENES EDITED INTO MONOLOGUES **143**

APPENDIX B
RECOMMENDED BOOKS **179**

ABOUT THE AUTHOR

GLENN ALTERMAN is the author of *Street Talk: Original Character Monologues for Actors, Uptown, The Job Book: One Hundred Acting Jobs for Actors, The Job Book 2: One Hundred Day Jobs for Actors, What to Give Your Agent for Christmas, Two-Minute Monologues, Promoting Your Acting Career, Two Minutes and Under* (volumes 1 and 2), *Creating Your Own Monologue,* and *An Actor's Guide: Making It in New York. Street Talk, Uptown, The Job Book, The Job Book 2, Two Minutes and Under, Creating Your Own Monologue,* and *An Actor's Guide: Making It in New York City* were all featured selections in the Doubleday Book Club (Fireside Theater and Stage and Screen Division). Alterman is also the author of the book for *Heartstrings: The National Tour* (commissioned by the Design Industries Foundation for Aids), a thirty-five city tour that starred Michelle Pfeiffer, Ron Silver, Christopher Reeve, Susan Sarandon, Marlo Thomas, and Sandy Duncan.

Alterman's plays *Like Family* and *The Pecking Order* were optioned by Red Eye Films (with Alterman writing the screenplay). His play *Solace* was produced Off Broadway by Circle East Theater Company and has had several European productions. *Solace* was recently optioned for European television. *Nobody's Flood* won the Bloomington National Playwriting Competition as well as being a finalist in the Key West Playwriting Competition. *Coulda-Woulda-Shoulda* won the Three Genres Playwriting Competition. This play has been published in two separate editions of the Prentice Hall college textbook and has been produced several times around the country.

Other plays include *Kiss Me When It's Over* (commissioned by E. Weissman Productions) starring and directed by Andre DeShields, *Tourists of the Mindfield* (finalist in the L. Arnold Weissberger Playwriting Competition at New Dramatists), and *Street Talk/Uptown* (based on his monologue books), produced at the West Coast Ensemble. *Goin' Round on Rock Solid Ground, Unfamiliar Faces,* and *Words Unspoken* were all finalists at the Actor's Theater of Louisville. *Spilt Milk* received its premiere at the Beverly Hills Rep/Theater 40 in Los Angeles and was twice selected to participate in the Samuel French One-Act Festival. *Spilt Milk* has had over twenty productions, including most recently with Emerging Artists Theater Company in New York. *The Danger of Strangers* won Honorable Mention in both the Deep South Writers Conference Competition and the Pittsburgh New Works Festival and was a finalist in the George R. Kernodle ConteStreet. There have been over fifteen productions of *The Danger of Strangers*, including Circle Rep Lab, West Bank Downstairs Theater Bar (starring James Gandolphini from "The Sopranos"), Emerging Artists Theater Company's One-Act Marathon, and Vital Theater Company on Theater Row in New York. Alterman's work has been performed at Primary Stages, Circle in the Square Downtown, the Turnip Festival, HERE Arts Center, LaMama, at the Duplex, Playwrights Horizons, and at several theaters on Theater Row in New York, as well as at many other theaters around the country.

Alterman is one of the country's foremost monologue and audition coaches, having helped thousands of actors in their search and preparation of monologues for auditions, as well as creating their own material for solo shows. In 1994 Alterman created The Glenn Alterman Studio (www.glennalterman.com), and through its auspices, he has worked privately as a monologue/audition coach at colleges, universities, and acting schools all around the country. He has lectured and taught at such diverse places as the Edward Albee Theater Conference (Valdez, Alaska), Southampton College, Governors School for the Arts (Old Dominion University), The School for Film and Television, Western Connecticut State College, Star Map Acting School of Long Island, the Dramatists Guild, The Learning Annex, the Screen Actors Guild, and The Seminar Center and in the Boston Public School System.

He presently lives in New York City where he teaches and writes plays, books, and screenplays.

ACKNOWLEDGMENTS

Glenn Alterman wishes to thank the following for their help in writing this book: Circle East Theater Company (Michael Warren Powell, Artistic Director), Emerging Artists Theater Company (Paul Adams, artistic director), and Doug Barron (Plaza Desk Top Publishing).

He especially wishes to thank the following playwrights for their creative contributions to this book: Mathew Witten, Joe Pintauro, Lanie Robertson, Annie Evans, Ty Adams, Mary Sue Price, William M. Hoffman, Anthony Holland, Anastasia Traina, Matty Selman, Simon Fill, Jonathan Reuning, Phil Hines, Scott C. Sickles, Bashore Halow, and Ellen Lewis and of course to all the folks at Smith and Kraus Publishers, especially Marisa Smith and Eric Kraus.

NOTE: For consistency, the pronoun *he* is used throughout the book whenever *he* or *she* might be used. This is done simply for expediency and clarity. It is not the author's intention to alienate or offend either sex, and he apologizes to anyone offended.

Introduction

An audition monologue is a marketing tool. Its sole purpose is to help you win an audition, get you an agent, or showcase your acting skills to theater companies, directors, and producers. Monologues are an invaluable part of every actor's marketing arsenal. Just as you should have an up-to-date picture and résumé, you should have at least three or four (or more) well-rehearsed, ready-to-go monologues.

But finding and rehearsing the right monologue is not an easy task. Believe me, I know. While actively pursuing my acting career, I probably logged in hundreds of hours at the Lincoln Center Library and at the Drama Book Store in New York, going through hundreds of monologue books and scanning perhaps thousands of plays. I was looking for just the right monologue: a monologue that "spoke" to me; a monologue that said what I wanted to say, the way I wanted to say it. I was constantly looking for monologues that I could emotionally relate to, a character I could identify with, and a story that I felt compelled to tell. Like many other actors, I was looking for that "prefect audition monologue." The monologues that I found, that met up to my stringent requirements, I soon discovered were ones that were being done all the time by other actors; they were overused. Another problem, after finally finding monologues that I thought were great audition material for me, I'd sometimes find out from agents and casting directors that they felt my monologue wasn't "selling me." I soon discovered that finding the right monologue can sometimes be very subjective. How you view yourself and how others see you don't always mesh. Marketing yourself and finding the best audition material for yourself can sometimes be very tricky.

I began working with actors on their audition monologues about twelve years ago. At that point, I had written a few books of original monologues (for Smith and Kraus). Occasionally an actor would ask me to help them work on a monologue from one of my books. I found that I enjoyed working with actors and discovered I had a knack for helping them connect with monologues — and not only mine, but all kinds. Soon I began teaching monologue audition classes as well as continuing with one-on-one coaching. Eventually, I began to give monologue and audition seminars all around the country. Over the years I've worked with thousands of actors and have discovered many of the best ways to find, rehearse, and perform monologues for auditions.

About eight years ago, I began keeping a teaching journal. I'd mark down things that I felt were absolutely necessary for successful monologue auditions. I also included things that I felt actors should avoid at all auditions. Of course, talent and skill are the most important factors in every audition. But I have seen hundreds of talented actors sabotage themselves by not knowing how to effectively showcase their talent at an audition.

This book contains many of the lessons that I've learned over the years both as an actor and as a monologue audition coach. Aside from my own perceptions, I've included observations from casting directors, talent agents, directors, and other actors. I think you'll discover that seeing the monologue audition from their different points of view can be a real eye-opener.

I've included chapters with interviews from some of the top agents and casting directors in the business. What do casting directors really look for at a monologue audition? What is the first thing they're looking for when an actor enters the audition room? What do actors consistently do wrong at auditions?

What advice do casting directors have for actors that might help them win monologue auditions?

I've tried to cover every aspect of this subject. I've dealt with everything from marketing yourself to learning how and where to find monologues that sell you to the best ways to rehearse and perform at those auditions. Everything from entrances to exits at auditions is covered. Everything from what to say (and not to say!) to knowing how (and when!) to leave an audition. I've even looked into how to deal with those auditions where you felt you really screwed up (happens to all of us). And as an additional bonus, there are dozens of rarely done and, in many cases, never-performed monologues included in this book.

When I finished writing the manuscript for this book, I gave copies of it to about a half a dozen casting directors and talent agents, as well as to several experienced actors, for their comments and feedback. I wanted to be sure to include everything anyone would need to know on this subject. Their comments were positive, and any suggestions that they made that I felt were valid were included in the final draft of this book.

I feel confident that *The Perfect Audition Monologue* can be of use to every actor, no matter where you are in your career. My intention in writing this book was to help actors deal with that dreaded thing called the monologue audition. Hopefully, after reading it, you'll find that your next audition won't be quite as stressful.

Have a good career, stay focused, and *never* give up on your dream!

Glenn Alterman

How to Get the Most out of This Book

This book is written for both the actor new to monologue auditioning as well as the seasoned pro who's been auditioning for decades. To get the most out of this book I suggest that you *don't* read through it nonstop from cover to cover. First look through the contents; see what stands out. Look for those things that interest you at the moment. Then skim through the book, stopping at particular chapters that you feel are pertinent to your needs or interest right now. For instance, if you'd like to learn is how to edit a monologue from a play, go to chapter 5. If you're interested in the best ways to prepare for an upcoming monologue audition, go to chapter 8.

After you've read through those particular chapters, I suggest that you *then* read through the entire book, taking notes or highlighting those things that you find apply to your particular situation.

Once you've started rehearsing your monologue and gotten it up on its feet, if you're having problems, refer to the chapters dealing with the basics and see where you may have gone off. Before your audition, you may want to reread the agent/casting director interview sections again for specific audition advice. You may find some value (and solace) in rereading some of the experiences of other actors in chapter 12. It's always comforting to know that you're not alone in your apprehension of auditioning. You'll discover that many others have met the challenge and gone on to successful careers.

Once you've finished reading the book, put the information you've learned into practical use. Go out there and prove to yourself that all this information can and will work for you.

This book is meant as a starting point, a launch pad for your future monologue auditions. Refer to it as often as you need, before every audition if necessary. Depending on where you are in your acting career, you may not feel the need to apply every rule in this book to the way you work on monologues. If something you've learned *before* reading this book still works for you, continue using it. If it's not broke, don't fix it. But always leave room for the possibility of discovering new ways to work, things that you can add on to what has worked for you in the past.

I wrote this book not only to instruct, but also to inspire. The point of the book is to show that actors can learn how to work on monologues in a way that will increase their confidence and help them win auditions. Once you develop confidence in any skill, fears can be alleviated. With any audition there is always some tension, some apprehension; that's only normal, accept it. But I believe that by learning how to challenge the fear (with knowledge and insight), you'll find that you can actually enjoy the monologue audition experience and maybe end up winning the game.

chapter 1

The Purpose of the Audition Monologue

WHAT IS A MONOLOGUE?

Dictionaries define *monologue* as a dramatic soliloquy or a long speech. In a play, a monologue is an uninterrupted speech. There are many types of monologues. Some are spoken directly to the audience. Others try to create the impression that the actor is alone, talking to himself. Some monologues occur when the character is talking to another person or group of people. There is another group of monologues where the character is talking to an imaginary person. The character may be saying things that he's always wanted to say but didn't get the chance or have the courage to say, or perhaps may be preparing to say into the future.

THE REASON FOR A MONOLOGUE AUDITION

The reason that casting directors, agents, and theater companies request a monologue audition is to give them some idea of your talent as an actor. Monologue auditions are used to cast plays, for theater company auditions, for auditions for college theater departments, and lately even for movie auditions.

One of the reasons actors have trouble performing monologues for auditions is that the audition monologue is an "unnatural" thing. Monologues from plays were never intended to be performed as audition material; that is not why the playwright wrote them. The purpose of the monologue in the play was to tell the playwright's story. Cutting monologues from plays has to be done judiciously. The monologue may work very well in the world of the play but trying to make it stand on its own as an audition piece may not create the effect you want.

WHAT CASTING DIRECTORS ARE THINKING DURING THE MONOLOGUE AUDITION

I've interviewed many casting directors for this book. One of the questions that I asked was what kind of things went through their minds during the monologue audition. Here are some of their replies.

- What is my first impression of this actor?
- How does he present himself? How does he look?
- Can he speak properly? Does he speak with a regionalism, a dialect?
- As he does his monologue, can he create a believable character?
- Does he make the dialogue believable, or does he sound phony?
- Does he seem confident or nervous?
- Does his monologue seem overrehearsed?

- Does he have stage presence?
- How does he move? Is he comfortable with his body?
- Does he seem comfortable on a stage performing?
- What kind of personality does he have? Does he seem friendly, accessible, professional?
- Will I be able to work with this actor? Do I feel that the director or other members of the cast will have any problems working with this actor?

WHY DO ACTORS NEED AUDITION MONOLOGUES?

Bottom line, the audition monologue is an important marketing tool that can get you a job or an agent or can give interested auditors some sample of your talent as an actor. Every actor's arsenal should include several well-rehearsed monologues, a good headshot, and a neat, well-organized résumé.

New monologues should be added to your repertoire on a regular basis. Monologues get stale from over use. If you discover that the monologue that you're using is being done a lot by other actors, you may want to find new pieces that aren't as popular. I recently saw a casting director at an audition silently mouthing the words of an overused monologue along with the actor up on the stage auditioning. It's not a terrible thing to do an overused monologue, especially if you've personalized it and made it your own, but there is a slight handicap if the auditors have heard the piece dozens of times. There are thousands of monologues out there to choose from: Why do material that everyone else is doing? One of the things that you want to do at an audition is entertain the casting director, not bore him with the same old stuff.

At its best, the monologue audition is an appetizer of your talent. It's a two-minute presentation of your talent, taste, and your skill. You want to find material that excites you, that you enjoy performing. You want to go to each monologue audition with enthusiasm, both about yourself as an actor and about the material that you've selected to perform for the audition. Throughout your career, you constantly audition for roles, hoping to get the part. Selecting a monologue is a proactive challenge. Here, you are in charge. You're not waiting for anyone to give you anything. Here you have control of what you want to perform and decide how you want to perform it.

SCENARIO ONE: ACTORS WHO LOVE TO DO MONOLOGUE AUDITIONS

For some actors, monologue auditions are just another chance to show their stuff. They relish each audition as a golden opportunity. They love to act and feel that here is a chance to do just that. They approach each audition with a great deal of enthusiasm, a " I can't wait to show 'em" excitement. They look at each monologue audition as an invaluable opportunity to meet new casting directors and directors. They think of auditions as an opportunity to show industry people how talented they are, how enthusiastic they are, how professional they are. From my experience, the actors in this bliss-filled category are, unfortunately, in the minority.

SCENARIO TWO: ACTORS WHO DON'T — AND I MEAN REALLY DON'T — ENJOY DOING MONOLOGUE AUDITIONS

For a great many actors, the monologue audition is a stress-filled, sometimes terrifying experience. Dry mouth, sweaty hands, anxiety, tension. To these actors, the audition seems like some Kafkaesque nightmare. You find yourself standing in a tiny room or on a huge theater stage, alone, being stared at by several strangers, as you try to perform a segment of a play that in all actuality was never meant to be performed as an audition monologue in the first place.

When you first enter the room, you're not quite sure what to say to these strangers, so you mumble a somewhat incoherent "hi." You muster up a generic smile, and then quickly look for a chair to sit and perform your monologue — since you've only rehearsed the monologue seated. But to your shock, horror, and dismay, you discover that there is no chair for you to use, so you quickly decide to do the monologue standing, something you've never done before. And so, apprehensively, you begin. Perhaps for the first time since infancy, you become aware, almost fixated, on your hands, which start moving wildly in space as you talk. You feel like your feet have become cemented to the floor; your body feels like lead. The lights in the room have suddenly become blindingly bright. Your voice, you notice, has gone up about three octaves.

At home when you rehearsed this very same monologue, you were so *there,* so inside the character, so —! But now, alone on that stage, you feel like you're delivering something like the Gettysburg Address, but in someone else's voice, to a group of disinterested strangers who couldn't care less about you or your burning desire to be an actor. After what seems like an hour or two, you finally finish the monologue. You quickly smile another generic smile, whisper "thank you very much" (trying desperately to sound sincere), and then flee from the room as quickly as your rubbery legs can carry you to a door, which you pray is the one that you entered from and not a broom closet. The audition is over; the humiliation is complete. You start to think that perhaps a career as an accountant might not be so bad. You go home, go to your room, sulk for a while, and then, well, start rehearsing a comedic monologue for tomorrow morning's audition. You decide that you will not let that day's harrowing experience get you down. You stand up, yell, "Hell no, I won't quit, never!" You're an actor. Tomorrow is another day, another chance, another audition. Maybe tomorrow's audition won't be so frightening.

GETTING AN AGENT

Before discussing the different monologue auditions, it might be helpful to briefly discuss the best ways to get an agent. There's no doubt that having an agent can sometimes make things a bit easier for an actor. But don't feel that just because you presently don't have an agent you can't make major strides in your career. By being proactive, focused, and diligent, actors can still have healthy careers without an agent. That being said, here are the best ways to get one.

GET A RECOMMENDATION FROM A CASTING DIRECTOR

A casting director who knows your work is certainly the best way to meet an agent. Casting directors are in daily contact with agents. When working on a specific project with a casting director, the agent suggests actors from his agency that might be right for roles in the play that the casting director is working on. Agents need to keep their relationships strong with the casting directors they work with. If a casting director asks the agent to meet with you (a referral), you can generally be certain the agent will oblige. Obviously you should know the casting director well before asking them for a referral. The casting director should be familiar with your work either by having seen you perform or (at the very least) having seen your work at auditions. When asking for a casting director's help, be professional and courteous. If he says no to your request, let it go, don't pursue the matter any further. The only thing that'll do is alienate you from him (and future potential work). When you meet with the agent, you should be at your best. The casting directors name and reputation go along with every referral he makes.

GET RECOMMENDATIONS FROM ACTORS
YOU'VE WORKED WITH

Actors you've worked with in shows or with whom you've taken classes can also introduce you to their agents. Make sure that the actor believes in you and your potential. Perhaps he's complimented your work in the past. If he agrees to arrange a meeting for you with his agent, ask what he feels would be the best way for you to make the contact. Would he feel comfortable calling his agent on your behalf? Or should you call his agent and use his name? Or (least preferable) should you send a picture and résumé including his name in your cover letter? If the actor refuses your request for a referral, let it go; it's not worth pursuing. He might have his own issues (insecurities, jealousy).

HIRE A NETWORKING FACILITY

Companies called networking facilities offer agent/actor introductions and auditions for a small fee You are not guaranteed anything from this arrangement other than the opportunity to meet with an agent or casting director. What's implied in this type of meeting is that if the agent likes you and believes in you, you might be able to work with their agency in the future.

SEND OUT PICTURES AND RÉSUMÉS

Sending unsolicited material to agents is one way to get their attention. The agent may see something in your photo that interests him and then call you in for a general interview/ audition. You should be aware that there is a lot of work involved in doing these mailings. If you don't have the time for this, you may want to hire a company that provides these services.

WALK THE PAVEMENT

Making the rounds, as it's commonly called, is another way to meet agents. It's probably the least successful way, since today many offices have security intercoms on their doors, and you won't be able to gain entry unless you're buzzed in. Generally, actors who stop by without an appointment are asked to either leave their photos in a basket outside the door or slip them under the door. There are, however, still some agents whose offices are accessible. It might be worth a try, especially on a nice spring day.

TYPES OF MONOLOGUE AUDITIONS

FOR AGENTS

You have been notified by the talent agent's office that the agent would like to meet with you for a general. Usually they'll ask you to prepare one or two monologues for the interview. Hopefully, you have a couple of well-rehearsed monologues ready to go. If not, you may have to really move on this. If the interview is a week or so away, you have sufficient time to get this together. If it's tomorrow, you're in trouble. In that type of situation it's best to see if you can schedule the appointment for a later time when you feel you'll be ready. An agent appointment is too valuable an opportunity to squander by just throwing something together overnight. You don't want your office monologue audition to be about trying to remember what the next line in the monologue is.

FOR CASTING DIRECTORS

Some casting directors have general interviews where they meet new talent. This is a far less common then agent interview. Generally casting director's meet new actors at auditions that they've held for particular projects. The casting director will occasionally be willing to see an actor that an agent has highly recommended, or, in some cases, from a photo that an actor had previously mailed to the casting director. At these interviews the actor is usually asked to prepare one or two brief monologues. These interviews are generally held in the casting directors office, but can be held at a theater that the casting director is connected to.

FOR THEATER COMPANIES

Once or twice a year many theater companies hold general auditions to cast roles for their upcoming year. Actors Equity requires that New York Equity resident companies hold these auditions to meet union members for future casting consideration. In some cases the theater company already has a resident company but might still be looking for a particular type for a role in an upcoming play. In other cases, there is no resident company, so all casting is done through agent submissions, casting director suggestions, and EPA's (Equity Principle Auditions). In some cases, sides from planned upcoming plays are used at the auditions, but quite often the actor is asked to prepare either a brief monologue or two contrasting monologues. Monologues that are similar in mood or theme to upcoming plays are recommended for the audition.

FOR A SPECIFIC PLAY

A play has been written and optioned and is now being produced. The production may be headed for a theater on Broadway, Off Broadway, Off-Off Broadway, or just about anywhere that someone decides that his play can be performed and an audience might come see it, such as churches, stores, basements — you name it. For the audition, the director (or casting director) decides whether to have actors read directly from the play — giving them sides in advance — or whether they should prepare a short monologue. If they want a monologue, they'll request material that is appropriate for the type and genre of the play.

FOR FILM

Nowadays many film companies (particularly the independents) are requesting that actors bring in a short monologue for their first audition. Rather than giving the actor sides to read from their planned film, they allow the actor to choose material that he feels shows off his capabilities. When selecting material for these types of auditions, choose something that doesn't require much movement. Also, the material shouldn't be too emotionally explosive. When performing the monologue, if you're supposed to be speaking directly to another character, be sure to use the camera as that character.

FOR CLASSROOM WORK

In acting class, a teacher will assign a particular monologue to an actor to work on a particular skill. For instance he may assign a monologue that demands certain emotions that he feels the actor has trouble expressing. Monologues are also used in class to stretch acting muscles. Actors use monologues to explore different acting styles or to investigate the works of playwrights that they might not have a shot at in the commercial world.

chapter 2

Before You Get Started

Before you start selecting audition material, you need to know your type and how you plan on marketing yourself. As I've mentioned, audition monologues are marketing tools whose only purpose is to get you a job or an agent. You can only select appropriate material if you know what type you are and how you're perceived in the marketplace. The monologue you select should exemplify your best attributes. This is not the time to stretch, to show them how well you can play older characters or how well you can do an Irish accent. These monologues should show the *best you — right now.*

MARKETING YOURSELF AS AN ACTOR

How you market yourself as an actor can be a crucial part of success in show business, especially at the beginning of a career. Many actors spend years focusing their energy on the craft, the artistry of being an actor. While that's certainly admirable, it's just not all there is. I have worked with many talented students who don't have a clue about how to market themselves or deal with the business side of show business. Talent agents, casting directors, and producers are all businesspeople. As an actor you have to learn to play the game.

According to Lee K. Bohlen, a professional life coach who holds workshops for actors, "Actors must think of themselves as a product. Once they do, they must then figure out the marketplace they want to sell their product —themselves — to. They must figure out a way that they can do this most effectively. One of the problems is that many actors think successful marketing is simply developing your craft. They take acting classes, dance classes, singing classes, etc., and feel that if they're well trained, they'll just be 'discovered.' That, quite often, is just a myth. They forget that this is a business, an industry. They leave out the part about being a businessperson. Actors must specify where they really want to go in their careers."

Quite often, while working with actors, I'll ask them about their goals, where they want to go in their career. Many of them tell me that they kind of *want it all*. I try to make them realize that that may happen eventually, but the best way to go about getting it all is to focus on one aspect of show business at a time. If you love theater, put your energy into succeeding in that arena first. Do what it takes to advance your theatrical career. Take classes, do targeted mailings, go to open calls, perhaps go to networking facilities to meet the agents and casting directors who can facilitate work in the theatrical field.

Believe me, there isn't enough time in the day to do all the things you could possibly do to advance yourself in a theatrical career. Remember, there's Broadway, Off Broadway, regional theater, summer stock, and so on. The same is true of the energy necessary for work in film and television commercials. Each one of these entertainment fields, if pursued fully, could easily take up all your waking hours.

Many actors try to be all things to all people in the business. There is a sort of desperation, a willingness to sell out, no matter what it costs, just to get ahead. Why go to musical auditions if you know you're not a good singer and can barely dance? Why go to that audition for the lead in Hamlet if you've never had any classical training and have never done classical work before? What I'm talking about here is focus. You only have so much time in a day, in a career, in a life. The more you can focus on personal goals, on what's in your heart, the more likely you'll achieve your goals.

WHAT TYPE ARE YOU?

Lee Bohlen says, "Actors tend to stay in the place where casting directors and agents identify them. They are categorized as young mom, young leading man, business exec, etc. We all have qualities that are beneath these surface labels. For example, think about Jack Nicholson. You can think of all the roles that he's played, but there's one thing that he brings to everything he does. That one thing is his 'real type.' In Nicholson's case, that real type can be described as 'dangerous and violent.' It's something you see in all his work. He brings these qualities to everything he plays."

It is imperative to discover just what your real type is and then do everything you can to promote yourself with that in mind. What is unique about you both as an actor and as a person? Once you've discovered that, then everything — from the monologues you select to your headshots, your mailings, and the auditions you go to — should express that.

This is a business where actors are constantly typecast and pigeonholed. You'll need to find the balance between the way they categorize you and your specific goals. I've seen many actors adjust their hairstyles and wardrobes and even alter their personalities just to be accepted as a particular type. I realize that at some point, usually at the beginning of a career, you might feel the need to adjust to "their" predetermined categories. That's fine, if you don't sell out completely and make yourself over. It can be OK on a temporary basis. Book the job, and then find ways to express your individuality within the confines of what is *professionally appropriate*.

Casting director Karen Kayser concurs that "in trying to be

all things to all people, actors make their biggest mistake, they come across as bland. One of the by-products of selling out totally to typecasting is that you lose some aspect of your uniqueness. And it is specifically that uniqueness that can land you on the top of the heap."

WHAT DO YOU WANT THEM TO SEE?
SELLING YOURSELF AS AN ACTOR

Hopefully by now you've started to grasp the importance of marketing yourself as an actor. But before you can start deciding which monologue is right for you, you may want to ask yourself: What do I want them to see? What am I *selling?*" When I ask actors these questions, quite often they'll give me a general answer like "I don't know, how talented I am I guess."

Duh! I think one of the main reasons actors select inappropriate audition monologues is because they haven't really looked at what they're trying to *say* with the material that they've selected. You are not only being evaluated on your talent but also on your aesthetic, your taste. One thing auditors are looking for at auditions is how appropriate the material that you've selected for yourself is. Your choice of material says so much about you. It gives them a sense of who you believe you are, both as a person and as an actor. So many actors are too cavalier about their monologue choices. If you're an actress in your early twenties, fair and delicate looking, with a soft voice and gentle personality, then choosing a monologue that shows a hardened woman with a foul mouth and a vile temper is inappropriate.

Actors constantly select monologues for the wrong reasons. They like the way the character speaks, the style of the writing, the subject matter, the play that the monologues come from. Although these things are important, they don't answer the most important question: Does this monologue sell who I am as an actor? By performing it at auditions, will they get some sense of my talent and who I am?

EXPERIENCE, ASSETS, AND LIMITATIONS

Another thing to keep in mind when looking for material is your training and life experience. If you're just starting out and haven't had much training, I suggest that you find material that you can understand, are comfortable with, and can relate to. Occasionally inexperienced actors choose material that makes emotional demands that they're not prepared to play: the characters are too complex, or the language is heightened. Although a monologue like this may be of some value in an acting class, it is the wrong choice for auditions.

I understand that some actors actually use auditions they don't care much about as a place to try out new monologues to see if they work. I don't think this is a good idea. Casting directors have long memories. Blowing an audition by trying out inappropriate material is a move that you may regret years later.

YOUR PERSONAL TASTE

When you select audition monologues, go with your first impulse. I recently heard Kathy Bates say that when she reads a script she goes with her stomach to help her decide about the material. There's something to be said for that. Sometimes actors second-guess themselves rather than going with their gut reaction. As you look through monologue material, try to stay open and allow the material to affect you. No one is a better judge of what moves you than you. Here is one of the few opportunities in your career where you are totally in charge of what *you* want to work on. The monologue that you select should move you, affect you, excite you. It should be material that motivates you. It should be material that you can't wait to get up and perform. And don't forget, it should be material that *can sell you and show them what you got!*

chapter 3

Finding the Right Monologues

HOW MANY MONOLOGUES WILL YOU NEED?

I suggest that at the very least, actors should have at least *four prepared audition monologues*. You'll need a comedic, a dramatic, a classical, and a poetic and/or surreal monologue.

The thing that I find interesting and difficult about finding comedic monologues is that people have difference senses of humor. Some people find Neil Simon's material funny; some don't. Some find Joe Orton or Nicky Silver's work hilarious; others don't. For that reason I generally suggest having two styles of comedic monologues in your prepared arsenal. One that is more mainstream, like a Neil Simon monologue. And one that is more out there, cutting edge, dark, like Christopher Durang or perhaps Nicky Silver.

Dramatic material for some reason seems more universal. Themes like the death of a child, father-son monologues, or mother-daughter material will generally affect a wide range of people in a similar way. You can assume that if the material you've selected emotionally engages you, it'll probably affect the auditors as well. But you can never really predict how someone will react. The same monologue that brought tears to the eyes of the auditors at one audition may be boring to the auditors at the next. Like everything else, some folks will like it and some won't. That being the case, you might as well select material that you find engaging, interesting, and enjoyable.

You should constantly be adding new material to your monologue arsenal. Don't wait until you find yourself going on automatic pilot at an audition. Keep adding and rotating new material. The more monologues you have, the more you'll have to choose from.

MONOLOGUE MISTAKES

What follows are some of the most common mistakes that actors make when selecting monologue material. I've gathered this list from years of seeing actors shoot themselves in the foot by picking inappropriate material and sometimes blowing their auditions.

- *Monologues inappropriate for your age range.* It's very important to find material that expresses your age range. An actor may be twenty-eight years old, but if he looks and sounds like someone in his early twenties, he should find material that expresses that. As a rule of thumb, try to keep within a five-year period of your real age.

- *Past-tense, narrative, expositional monologues.* Nothing is more boring at an audition than a monologue with a lot of unnecessary background information and exposition. As a child, your parents may have read you bedtime stories. Those stories were filled with exposition and narrative. The reason they're called bedtime stories is they put you to sleep. Monologues with too much exposition and past-tense narrative will have the same effect on the auditors. You generally have about two minutes to impress the auditors. Filling that time with material filled with past-tense narrative is not the best choice. Try to find emotional, present-tense, active, conversational material for your auditions.

One more word about memory monologues: Some monologues, although they are past tense and narrative, have a strong emotional punch. At one time many male actors were doing the last monologue from *I Never Sang for My Father*. Many men related to the theme of father-son alienation. Memory monologues that emotionally affect you and allow you to showcase deep feelings are good choices for monologue auditions.

- *Stale monologues.* When a monologue is no longer fun to do at an audition, when it no longer engages you, it's time to dump that sucker in the recycle bin. Yes, you may have loved it at one time, but if you find yourself performing it on automatic pilot, move on to new material.

- *Poorly edited monologues.* Sometimes actors try to *force* sections of dialogue from a play into an audition monologue. There are several reasons that this may not work. First, the logic of what the dialogue is about may not make sense as a monologue. What that other character in the scene is adding to the conversation may be important. Cutting that information may make the edited monologue confusing. The playwright didn't intend his material to be performed as an audition monologue. There may be a rhythm to the dialogue that is broken when it is cut and pasted into a monologue. Actors will find themselves frustrated when working on mismatched material and generally will blame themselves and their acting rather than the real culprit here, the editing.

- *Monologues without any emotional punch.* As a general rule of thumb, if the material engages you it will engage them. You want to find monologues that move and excite you.

- *Emotionally overwrought monologues.* Doing monologues that require you to have a complete emotional catharsis in two minutes can be excruciating for both you and the auditors. We've all been at those auditions where you can hear an actor's loud cries and screams coming from the audition room. This kind of display, especially in those small rooms, can be embarrassing and intolerable. Out of respect, most casting directors won't stop you but will certainly want to. Remember, the point of general auditions is for the casting director to get to know *you*. Screaming, yelling, and agonizing for two minutes is not the you you want them to know.

- *Monologues without any emotional transition.* Try to find material that allows you to show a variety of emotion. Unfortunately, many monologues from plays express only one intense emotion. The character may be having an angry tirade or a painful breakdown, but after about a minute or so of that, we need to see something else, some other emotions. Remember, this is an audition, a showcase of you and your talent; don't limit it by playing only one emotion.

- *"Done to death" monologues.* There are certain monologues that it seems *everyone* is doing. Sometimes they're from plays that are currently being performed on Broadway. Recently, because of its popularity, I've noticed many young women performing the same monologues from the Broadway play *Proof*. In general, try to find material that isn't done to death. Remember, part of what you want to do at an audition is *entertain* the casting director. By performing new and exciting material, you'll have the advantage of having a more captive audience.

- *Monologues that can't stand on their own.* Some monologues can only be enjoyed if you know the background material from the play from which they came. Important references within the monologues only make sense to the listener if he knows the context from which they came. Monologues that can't stand on their own will only confuse the auditors and focus them not on your audition but on trying to comprehend the story you're trying to tell.

- *Inappropriate monologues.* It only makes sense to do monologues that are similar in genre and mood to the play that you're auditioning for. If you're auditioning for a David Mamet play, it's inappropriate to do your Neil Simon monologue, even though you love doing it. Have something in your monologue arsenal that's more appropriate in feeling and sensibility to the Mamet play.

- *Monologues that are too long.* When they say they want a monologue that is two minutes or under, that's what they mean. It can only annoy them if your material is clocking in at four minutes and they have to sit there and listen. Not knowing how long your monologue runs is no excuse; time it at home.

  If the only appropriate material that you have for the audition runs four minutes, be prepared to be cut off (and be gracious when you are). Don't ever rush your audition just to meet a time limit. It's better to show them two minutes of quality work and be cut off, than speed through four minutes worth of material just to meet the time requirement.

- *Offensive material.* Offensive language and sexually explicit material is not appropriate for most auditions. By choosing that kind of material, you'll stand a good chance of offending the auditors and turning them off to you, even if you give a good audition. There are, however, some plays that this material is appropriate for, but you'd better be certain that off-color monologue is appropriate before you bring it in. It's never smart to select monologues that in any way describe or discuss animal or child torture or mutilation.

- *Material that stretches you.* Auditioning is not the time to show them your entire range as an actor. Just because you think you can play a character much older than you, this is not the time to do it (save it for class). What they want is to see is material that shows them you, right now.

- *Star-identified material.* Try not to do a monologue that has a particular actor's stamp on it; you're only setting yourself up for comparison.

- *Monologues in dialect.* It's generally not a smart idea to do an audition in a dialect. If you accidentally drop out of the dialect, even for a word or two, you'll lose some believability. If the play that you're auditioning for is written in a dialect, and they've requested that you do the audition with a dialect, then of course you should.

- *Monologues with whiny, negative characters.* Unless the character in the play that you're auditioning for is negative and whiny, it's always better to find material in which the character overcomes some adversity. This is not a hard, fast rule, but one that might get you some extra points at the audition. Everyone likes to see a winner or at least a character that is trying to overcome something.

NONTRADITIONAL MATERIAL SELECTION

There is no reason why an African American should only limit himself to material about the black experience. If you can emotionally relate to the character, there is no reason why you shouldn't be able play him. Actors of all ethnicities occasionally limit their choice of material because the character as written in the play is not the same ethnicity as they are. I feel that this is wrong and only promotes negative stereotyping in casting. I'm a strong believer in nontraditional casting. If the material moves you, excites you, engages you, give it a shot, see how it feels, even if the character is not the same color as you.

chapter 4

Source Material for Monologue Auditions

Actors can find material appropriate for monologue auditions from many sources. Where and how you select monologues depends on your personal taste, the type of monologue audition, and accessibility to the source. What follows are descriptions of each monologue source and its pros and cons.

MONOLOGUES FROM PLAYS

By far the most common source of monologue material for auditions is from plays, mostly published plays. Actors can edit the monologue directly from a scene, or can edit several speeches together to create a monologue. (See chapter 5 for tips on editing a monologue from a play.)

Occasionally, actors select monologues from unpublished plays in which they created a role, perhaps in a showcase production. One of the advantages in finding monologues from unpublished plays is that no one else will have the material.

THE PROS

- Published plays are the most common source for audition monologue material. They are easily available at bookstores and libraries.
- Some auditions specifically request material be from published plays.
- By reading the entire play, you may discover insights (and motivations) into the character.
- In a play the given circumstances are established in the story. You then only have to adapt and personalize them to your audition situation.
- Many actors feel more grounded in material from plays since they know the background information.

THE CONS

- The monologue from the play was not written to be performed as an audition piece.
- There may be too much exposition in the monologue to make the material workable as an audition piece. You always want to perform a monologue that is active and emotionally engaging, not expositional.
- The auditors may be confused by a selected monologue from a play because they might need to know the entire play to understand what the character is talking about.
- Many play monologues don't have an emotional arc. Quite often only one emotion (such as anger) is expressed throughout the entire piece. You always want to find material that expresses emotional range and versatility.
- Actors sometimes find it difficult to edit monologues from plays. They may inadvertently cut the muscle not the fat from the material. (See chapter 5, "Editing the Audition Monologue.")

MONOLOGUES FROM MOVIES

These monologues are edited directly from motion picture scripts. There are a couple of compilations of movie monologues. One book that I recommend is *The Actor's Book of Movie Monologues,* edited by Marisa Smith and Amy Schewel (Smith and Kraus). You can also rent a videotape of a film and then transcribe a monologue directly from the film.

THE PROS

- The actor, after having seen the movie, may have been so moved by the monologue that he may be inspired to perform the material himself.

- Generally, movie dialogues and monologues are written concisely, without too much exposition — a plus for audition material.

- Movie monologues are not done that often, so there's less concern about the material being overdone.

THE CONS

- Some movie monologues are associated with a particular actor in a movie. If the auditors are familiar with the film (and identify it with a particular actor's performance), you're setting yourself up for comparison.

- It is more difficult to find movie monologues since most films have few if any monologues in the script.

- For some monologue auditions, movie monologues are not acceptable.

- Many movie voice-over monologues are not good audition material. Even though the particular voice-over may have been effective in the movie, you were visually engaged while listening to it. The images in the scene may have been part of what moved you.

- The camera sometimes adds emotional impact to the material (such as close-ups and so on), which obviously won't be there to enhance your audition performance.

- Sometimes during a movie monologue, music or sound effects (sometimes very subtle) are added to enhance the emotional impact of the monologue. Obviously, you won't be bringing an orchestra in for background music during your audition.

ORIGINAL AUDITION MONOLOGUES

These are monologues specifically written to be performed by actors for auditions. They generally try to meet all the requirements necessary for monologue auditions (two minutes and under, succinct dialogue, and so on). There are quite a few books of these kinds of monologues. I personally have written five books of original monologues, most recently, *Two Minutes and Under, Volume 2* (Smith and Kraus.)

THE PROS

- They generally run the proscribed time for auditions, two minutes and under.

- There are no plays to read; what you see is what you get.

- You can interpret this material more freely, more personally. You can use more of yourself and your imagination in creating the given circumstances.

- These monologues are specifically written to be performed as audition material; they cater to the actor's needs in an audition.

- They generally will have an emotional arc, less exposition, and a clean beginning, middle, and end.

- This material cannot be identified with a well-known actor from a play or movie.

- A few casting directors request that you only do material from plays.

- Some actors need more background information to be able to work on a character.

- If you're stumped or blocked on your work on the material, you're on your own; there's no other source material.

MONOLOGUES FROM LITERATURE

These are monologues that are found primarily in novels but can also be found in newspaper or magazine articles. Sometimes while reading a book a certain passage moves you. The monologue may be a touching description of something that the character has experienced or is presently seeing. Material written in the first person singular can often be turned into excellent monologue material. Dialogue in the novel can also be edited to create an effective audition monologue. There are a few books of monologue selections from literature. I recommend *Monologues from Contemporary Literature, Volume 1,* edited by Eric Kraus (Smith and Kraus).

THE PROS

- Generally you have a great deal of background material on your character in a novel.

- Characters in novels can be fleshed out a great deal more than in a play.

- The writing can be top-notch.

THE CONS

- Some casting directors only want to see material from plays.

- Sometimes literary material doesn't translate well into effective, emotionally engaging audition material.
- A beautiful narrative section from a novel may be too passive and won't make for engaging audition material.
- If the casting director has read the novel, he may have his own picture of the how character should be portrayed. Your interpretation (as well as your physical presence) may not be how he sees the character.

MONOLOGUES FROM TRIAL TRANSCRIPTS AND PUBLIC HEARINGS

This is material culled from courtroom transcripts, interviews, and public hearing transcripts. As we know from many of the well-publicized trials, such as the O. J. Simpson trial, the Menendez case, and the Meg Ryan stalker case, dramatic testimony is often given. This testimony can be transformed into dramatic monologue material.

THE PROS
- You might find some very dramatic, high-charged material.
- This type of material is rarely done at auditions.
- Because the dialogue is actual testimony, it has the ring of authenticity. It sounds naturalistic and might be easier to say.
- To some casting directors, it might seem brave for an actor to attempt this kind of material.

THE CONS
- Some casting directors only want to see material f rom plays.
- Courtroom transcripts are sometimes difficult to get.

- It may be difficult to edit this kind of material and make it work as a successful monologue.
- Much of this material is expositional, which is not usually good for monologue auditions.
- Because you're dealing with well-known people in the media, you're setting yourself up for comparison. This is especially true if the trial was televised and viewed by a large audience.

WRITING YOUR OWN AUDITION MATERIAL

Some actors write their own monologues for auditions. They customize their material to exhibit their acting skills. In some cases the material is autobiographical, based on true incidents from their own life. Sometimes actors create fictional characters that they know they can identify with and portray. If writing your own monologue or one-person show interests you, please check out my book, *Creating Your Own Monologue* (Allworth Press).

THE PROS

- You have total control of the material and can make revisions based on your own needs and whims.
- With autobiographical material, you know the character inside out.
- The emotional connection with self-written material can be very engaging — both for you and the auditors.
- If you go up on your lines during the audition, it's easier to ad-lib until you find your place again.

THE CONS

- Many casting directors disapprove of self-written audition monologues.

- Your writing skills may not be as effective as you think they are.

- Ironically, because the character is some aspect of you, you may find it difficult to "play yourself."

- Although the material may be personal or emotionally engaging, it may not make for particularly strong audition material. It may resonate powerfully only to you, not to the auditors.

A NOTE ON INTERNET SOURCES

In the last few years a number of Internet sites have popped up offering actors free monologues. The material on these sites is either from movies, plays, or originals. All the actor needs to do is select material that appeals to him and then print a copy. To find some of these sites, just use the keyword *monologues* on your server. One of the better sites that I discovered was Colin's Movie Monologue Page (www.whysanity.net/ monos/).

chapter 5

Editing Monologues from Plays

BASIC RULES FOR EDITING SCENES INTO MONOLOGUES

There are some basic rules that you should try to adhere to when editing a section of a play into an audition monologue. From the onset, you should realize that the material was not originally written to be performed in this way, so you may have your work cut out for you. Remember, what you're attempting to do is *edit the material it in a way that will serve you as an audition piece to showcase your skills.*

First, you'll want to start off with a character that interests and engages you. You'll want the play to have dialogue that you're comfortable (and able) to say. You'll need to find a scene in the play that has the potential of being turned into an active audition monologue. One of the biggest mistakes occurs when actors, because of their determination to make a scene into a monologue, try to *force* the material into an unplayable monologue. Rehearsing this type of material will be an uphill battle.

You'll find yourself frustrated and blame your acting ability rather than the real culprit, the poorly crafted monologue. As you edit a scene (or sections) from a play into a monologue, keep the following things in mind:

- *The monologue should be about two minutes or under.* There are some auditions where a longer monologue is required. In those cases, the material may be a little longer (perhaps three minutes). There are also some auditions (not many, thank God) where they only want to see a one-minute monologue. When editing down to a one-minute monologue, you really have to cut to the bone; you literally can't waste a word.

- *The story of the monologue shouldn't be too complex or convoluted.* Your time at the audition is limited. You don't want to perform a monologue that's too confusing and calls more attention to it than you.

- *Try to edit out most of the exposition.* It tends to drag the piece down and will bore the auditors.

- *Sometimes all you have to do is cut the dialogue that the other person in the scene is saying.* If you have a line that is a reaction line to something the other character just said, cut it.

- *Ideally the monologue should have a clear beginning, middle, and end.* I realize that many monologues don't meet this requirement. All I can say is that creating a short monologue from a scene, with a complete journey, is easier for you to rehearse and perform and is more satisfying (and entertaining) for the auditors to watch.

- *You'll want a monologue that has an emotional arc, that shows some emotional range.* Some scenes in plays express only one or two strong emotions when edited into the monologue form. If all you want to show them is how well you play anger, there are plenty of monologues for that. Try to find material that shows off your strong and soft sides.

- *Unlike a play, a monologue doesn't always have to have conflict in it.* Strong characterization and dialogue are sometimes enough to make the monologue a good audition piece. But if you can find material where the character is in conflict and is fighting for something, you'll find that you have more to play and that the monologue is more engaging. Plays are about characters with conflicts. Find scenes that express the characters conflict; they'll make for better audition monologues.

- *A line that appears later in the play may be added to make the monologue work better.* Editing material from different sections of the same play can sometimes make for a more effective monologue. But be careful to keep the playwright's rhythms and intentions the same. The material should make sense logically and emotionally.

- *Sometimes dialogue in plays has a certain rhythm.* When these rhythms are interfered with, the material doesn't have quite the same resonance. As you rehearse the edited sections of dialogue, be aware if the rhythms seem off. If they are, see if you can reedit the material to make it work.

- *Always try to keep in mind what the playwright was trying to say.* You have an obligation to be truthful to the character and the basic truth of the play — its ideas and themes.

- *Think of your audition monologue as a miniature one-act play.* For examples of scenes edited into monologues, see Appendix A, page 143.

chapter 6

Rehearsing the Monologue

INITIAL WORK ON THE MONOLOGUE

The way that you work on your audition monologue is quite important. It can determine not only how effective your audition will be, but sometimes how long you'll be able to use the monologue before it becomes stale.

THE MISTAKE OF MEMORIZING FIRST

One of the most common mistakes actors make when starting out their work on audition monologues is to *memorize too soon.* They find a monologue that they like and instantly sit down to memorize it. Why? Once you memorize your monologue, your final performance is, to some degree, set. Before you've sufficiently explored the meaning of the material, or even what the character is really trying to say, you've preset the results. By early memorizing you cut out one of the most important and enjoyable parts of the rehearsal process — discovery. I know that many actors prefer to memorize first "to get the words out of the way." The question I often ask my students is, "When you begin work on new play, would you go to the first rehearsal on the first day with your part completely memorized?" Generally not. Then why approach monologue material that way? A monologue is, after all, a piece of theater.

The brain memorizes in sections, patterns. When you memorize right at the start, some of how you'll be saying the words in performance is preset. When we were children, we were taught the Pledge of Allegiance. We learned it by rote, the same way actors memorize their monologues. Consequently, we all say the pledge of allegiance exactly the same way — "I pledge allegiance . . . to the flag . . . of the United States of America . . . " Our inflection and pacing is the same.

That's how a monologue sounds when it is memorized too soon. You can sometimes tell when an actor has memorized his material too soon by the fixed way he performs it; there will be an unnatural quality to his read. Some actors think they can first memorize the words, then somehow layer on the emotions, and finally add the blocking. It sounds like they're layering and icing a cake, not rehearsing a monologue. Memorizing first is not an organic way to develop a role.

I'm making a big deal about memorizing because I've discovered many actors work this way. What I suggest is that you rehearse your monologue just like you would prepare for any other role in a play — in a step-by-step process of discovery. Generally, the memorizing part is the last thing you want to do after you've done all your discovery. You'll notice that when you finally do sit down to memorize, it'll be quick and effortless. This is because you've probably retained a lot of the words during your rehearsal process.

THE FIRST READ

Many actors try to "act" the character before they really know what they're doing. The best way to start your work on a new monologue is to *say the words*. Don't try to perform or dramatize them. Don't recite them; just say the words for you, *as you*. Say them the way you generally talk.

Notice any initial impulses, any feelings the material brings up in you. Any impulse that you have is valid, so go with it. If you have an urge to get up and move, do it. Don't question your initial response. This is a like a first date. Everything is fresh, new, possible. Try to comprehend what you're saying as you say it. *Stay in the moment with what you're saying.* If questions come up about why the character is saying a specific line, you might make a note to look at that at some point. What does the character mean by that phrase? Why does he use that particular word to express his feeling about something? Notice his thinking, his actions, how he strings thoughts together in a particular sequence. What does he mean?

After the initial read-through, put the monologue down and see what stays with you. See what ideas, feelings, impressions you have. Actors can discover a great deal in that first read. Occasionally, I'll ask students questions about the material. I'm always amazed at how much insight they've gained into the character from the first read. Those initial feelings and impulses are not to be discarded. They are the launch pad for your work on the monologue. They are the creative beginnings from which everything else will grow.

WORKING IMPROVISATIONALLY

Many actors like to do an improvisation after their first run-through. I think improvising can be very helpful while working on monologues. Put the monologue in your own words; try to express what you've learned from the text.

Select a person from your real life and use them as the imaginary other person to whom you're speaking. It's not important to communicate the facts to the other person, but rather the meaning of the material as you see and feel it.

SUBSEQUENT READ-THROUGHS

I like to think of the initial work on a monologue as analogous to dipping a white sheet in yellow dye. At the beginning, the sheet is pure white. After your initial read-through (the first dipping of the sheet), you have some first impressions, remnants of the character remain with you (some dye has attached itself to the sheet). After each subsequent read, you discover more and more about the character: with each dip of the sheet, more dye is absorbed. You also start to get a better sense of the journey of the monologue, of the story that's being told.

When rehearsing your monologue this way, try not to say the words over and over mechanically, but continually look into the character — his world, his thoughts, his feelings. A certain phrase might become the portal into who (for you) this character is. Even a single word in the monologue may give you the handle you're looking for.

It's as if after each read an inner landscape of who this character is starts to develop inside you. The character becomes a part of you. There is a place inside you that begins to see his world, understand his feelings, and identify with who he is. You'll be able to tap into this inner landscape when you perform the monologue. The character is no longer just a playwright's words on a page. You have an identity with the character, a symbiotic connection. This connection will make your version of this character different from anyone else's.

For those of you who like to work improvisationally, continue doing improvs of the material followed by readings of the actual text. Again blend your own words with the playwright's. If you continue this process of improvisations followed by reading the text, you'll discover that certain words, phrases from the text, have stuck with you. You'll start to *retain* sections of the monologue without actually sitting down and memorizing. You'll also notice that the text becomes *more your own*.

Eventually you'll be able to play the character completely from yourself. Going back to the dyed-sheet analogy, the white sheet has now become a rich yellow; you and the character are one.

The inner landscape of the complete character now lives within you. At the audition, after you've done your initial relaxation and preparation, all you have to do is focus your attention on that inner landscape, and the character will emerge from you in an effortless, organic way.

DISCOVERING AND CREATING YOUR CHARACTER

YOUR ACTOR'S IMAGINATION

I strongly believe that actors have an innate ability to create wonderfully personalized characters solely from their imaginations, without a lot of gimmicks and unnecessary exercises. Acting classes are important to an actor's growth as an artist, but I've discovered that sometimes actors overindulge in exercises or techniques learned in class. This can sometimes lead to heady, pedantic work. Please don't get me wrong: actors should study their craft. But what you learn in class must be processed and used in a creative way. An actor's imagination is the key to creating characters — and giving great monologue auditions. When you were very young, you could spend hours alone in your room playing with your soldiers or your dolls. You created whole worlds for yourself that you totally immersed yourself in, just for fun. Make-believe was exciting, engaging. You probably lost all track of time or where you were; you were in your imaginary world. Nobody had to tell you to act; you just did, for the fun of it. Unfortunately, as we get older, we hear our parents telling us to "Stop pretending! Grow up!" And so we do stop pretending and that wonderful *imaginary muscle* atrophies.

But at any time we choose, we can return to our imagination; we can rely on it in our acting work. Acting classes, sensory work, and the many available acting techniques can help us find ways to rediscover the world of innocent childlike imagination. But eventually all acting begins with the text. We must find the truth within the given circumstances. And the character we're trying to create comes from our imagination. As actors we have just one main responsibility — to be honest and truthful in our work; to make the playwright's character our own. This is true whether we are developing a character for a play, a movie, or an audition monologue.

You must bring yourself and your personal imagination to the character. Remember, I can always read the monologue myself; I don't need you to do that for me. Many actors give a dramatic reading of material. They give colorful line readings and generalized emotions. They're not fully engaged; there's always a distance between themselves and their work. What's really expected from you is your personal interpretation of the material. What can you bring to the table from your life experiences and your imagination? The more you can bring of yourself to your acting, the more specific your work will be.

THE SCRIPT AS A GUIDE

In most plays the playwright will include a character description on the first few pages. The setting of the play (monologue) will also provide clues. If your piece is set in a swanky Park Avenue apartment, and your character has lived there with his family all his life, then we'll have some idea about his background. He may have resented his wealth or totally enjoyed it. Another clue is the time period. Obviously a woman living in the 1700s would be different in many ways than a woman living in 2003. Ask yourself the following basic acting questions:

- Who am I?
- Where am I?
- Why am I there?
- What is it that I'm doing?
- Why am I doing it?

Look for revealing statements made by your character or by other characters about your character. Ask yourself these questions about the monologue:

- At what point in the story is this speech being delivered? Look at the moment before and after the monologue.
- Why is the character saying these words now?
- Who is he talking to? What is their relationship?
- What is the monologue about, what is the character trying to say?
- How do you think these words are affecting the listener(s)?
- What does your character want from the other character?
- Always keep in mind what is at stake. If your character doesn't get what he wants, what would he do?
- Is he telling the truth to the other person or is he lying to her and/or himself?

Once you've answered all these questions, you must start making personalized choices that will make the situation real for yourself.

WRITING THE CHARACTER'S BIOGRAPHY

Another way to explore a character is to write a biography about him. Based on what you've learned from the text, use your imagination to create an entire life for him. Start out by imagining where he was born, his childhood, what his life was like growing up, his likes and dislikes — everything that you need to know to make him real for you. Generally these biographies are only about a page or two, but if you get carried away, don't stop; write and explore until you're satisfied. Following are some biographical questions:

- How old is he?
- Where does he live? What is his place like? Describe it.
- What are his current circumstances?
- Is he single? Married? Does he have children, and if so, how does he relate to them?
- What is he like at home when no one else is around?
- What are his likes and dislikes?
- What are his favorite colors?
- What kinds of clothes does he wear?
- What was his childhood like? Describe his family life and upbringing.
- Does he believe in God? Is he religious?
- How does he see the world? What is his philosophy of life? Is he an optimist or pessimist?
- What are his politics?
- Is he social or a loner?
- How is his self-esteem? Is he a confident person?
- How do other characters speak about him?
- What kinds of things would make him laugh? Cry?
- What is the first impression someone would get when first seeing him?
- How does he speak? Slow or fast? Does he speak with a dialect? Does he have a speech impediment (such as a stutter)?
- What does his voice sound like — shrill, gravely, hoarse?
- Does he overindulge in alcohol or drugs?
- What does he do to entertain himself? Does he go to movies, plays, bars?

The questions can go on and on, but these should get you started.

OBJECTIVES AND OBSTACLES

Find the character's *objectives* in the monologue. What does your character want to achieve as a result of his actions? As you may know, you can have many objectives, both major and minor in a monologue: Ask yourself the following questions:

- Why is he saying what he's saying? What's his motivation?
- What does he want? What are his objectives?
- Why does he want this?

In a play (and monologue) the obstacles are what keep your character from accomplishing his objectives. Quite often they cause conflict between characters. See if this is apparent in your monologue. Characters may sometimes be having an internal or psychological struggle. Once you discover what your character wants, then ask yourself the following questions:

- What obstacles are getting in his way and preventing him from getting what he wants?
- Does he have a time limit to accomplish his objectives?
- Does he have the skills (the ability) to accomplish his objectives?
- Will he need to overcome fear or guilt before he can accomplish his objectives?

FIND THE BEATS

What your character does to accomplish each minor objective is called a beat. The beat is a unit of action, and each beat is a necessary step toward the major objective. You should always break down your monologue into beats. You should be able to state the objective and obstacle for each beat. Always ask yourself, either "What am I doing?" or "What must be done?" So often actors depend on generalized emotions to carry them through a monologue. Not only is this not a dependable way to work, it's not good acting.

chapter 7

Continuing Your Work: Preparing for the Monologue Audition

PERSONALIZING AND IDENTIFYING

You must always make all your acting choices personal. The more you can personally invest yourself into the character you're working on, the more effective your audition monologues (and all your acting work) will be. At auditions, auditors see many generic monologues. Actors, desperate to get a job, quite often play it safe in preparing their monologues. Rather than exposing a part of themselves in their work, they rehearse and perform in a *safe mode*. Rather than seeing what they have in common with a character, many actors play their characters the way they've seen other actors play similar characters. They'll play an *idea* of how they feel the character should be played. They work purely from their heads. These kinds of performances are pure surface. They are *play-acting* rather than truly engaging themselves in their character. They have not fully invested themselves in their characters.

IDENTIFYING WITH YOUR CHARACTER: TWO IMPORTANT QUESTIONS

Two questions I usually ask my students when they begin work on a new character are: How are you like this character? How are you not like this character? These questions can open up the exploration for your work. They help you to determine the road that you might need to travel from where you are now to where your character is. Since you're not the king of England or (I hope) you've never murdered or raped anyone, how do you play kings, rapists, and serial murderers? One way is by asking yourself: How am I like this character? How am I not like this character?

All you really have as an actor is yourself: your life experiences, your feelings, and your imagination. Even if the auditors have seen your monologue a hundred times, if you've personalized your work and truly identified in some personal way with the character that you're portraying, it will seem different from everyone else's.

I remember when we were casting my play *The Danger of Strangers*. The play is an erotic thriller. My ideas for the characters were Michael Douglas–Sharon Stone types. (*Basic Instinct* had recently been released.) We saw some very talented Michael Douglas–Sharon Stone types that day. An actor had recommended James Gandolphini for the Michael Douglas role. But James was very wrong for this role, no Michael Douglas he. (This was several years before his Sopranos fame.) He read with Susan Aston, who, although very talented, was not a Sharon Stone type. But the two of them gave a brilliant, personalized audition. I learned something very important that day. I thought I knew my play, my characters, what we were looking for. But James and Susan's personalized audition changed my mind completely. I thought my play was an erotic thriller about two people trying to get it on, but these two actors taught me that my play was really about two lonely people trying to connect. Naturally they both got the parts and were subsequently wonderful in the roles.

OUR MANY SELVES

All of us have many selves that live within us. There's the self that you are with your family, the self you are with your boyfriend or girlfriend, the self you are with a teacher in a class, the self you are when you're alone on a trip, and so on. They are all you, parts of you. These different selves can be of great use when working on new characters. Finding just the right part of you, the right self to use when working on a new character, can be a great way to honestly (and organically) portray a character that you're working on. Think about this when you're working on new material: you might find it a real eye-opener.

THE CHARACTER'S PHYSICAL LIFE

I've noticed that in many auditions, actors quite often choose to remain seated in the chair that's provided at the audition, even if being seated is totally inappropriate for the material that they're performing. (See "To Sit or Not to Sit During the Monologue Audition" later in this chapter.) Many actors act from the neck up. Their face, voice and, to some degree, hands are their only means of expressing themselves. They are talking heads. Characters, like people, have a physical life; they *move*. And not only do they move, they move in a very particular way.

The best way to work on a character's physical life is to allow your impulses to lead you. If you want to move around during the monologue, by all means — move! Let your body guide you as to how, when, and how much. You may get an urge to move in a specific way; trust it, even if it's not the way you usually move. You may discover a way of moving that's very specific to the character you're working on. If you try something and it doesn't feel right, don't repeat it during the next run-through. In your rehearsals, be brave, be outrageous, try things, keep trying things, but always be truthful and stay connected and in the moment. Don't make choices from your head, and try not to direct yourself.

GROUNDING YOURSELF IN YOUR OWN PERSONALIZED GIVEN CIRCUMSTANCES

Another way to personalize a monologue is to add your own given circumstances to the text. This is especially effective while working on original monologues. The following are a list of questions that will help you in developing your own personalized set of given circumstances. Some of these questions might seem similar to previous ones I've discussed in the last chapter, but you'll notice that the focus here is quite different; it's strictly on your imagination and your real world, not the world of the play.

- *Where are you?* Select a real place from your real life. The more familiar the place is to you, the better. Don't be satisfied with an answer like the house I once used to live in. Be specific. What room in that house? Specifically where are you standing in that room? Remember what the room looked like, where the clock was, the paintings, and so on. If the monologue that you're working on is from a play, select a place that works within the reality of the scene in the play. Try to find a place in your real life that corresponds to the scene in the play. Again, the more specific you are, the more effective this will be for you.

- *What time of year is it?* We behave differently on a cold winter day than on a hot and muggy summer night. Be specific as to the time of year; pick a month. Is it a cold day in February or a hot day in July? Again, if you're working on material from a play or movie, keep the time of year that you select truthful to the scene in the play.

- *What time of day?* Is it three in the morning or three in the afternoon? There are differences in how we respond to things at different times of the day.

- *What happened the moment before?* What happened right before you began doing the monologue? The motivation for the words that you're using in the monologue quite often comes as a response to what the other character just said or what just happened in the scene. If the monologue is from a play, look at what happened in the story right before your character started to speak. Once you discover that, personalize the moment before, make it real for you. Find a scenario from your real life that's similar to that moment. You might find it helpful to even write out what the other character just said to you. Use that personally scripted dialogue as part of your preparation each time you rehearse and perform the monologue. If you've never had anything like that happen to you, then use your imagination. Use the magic "if."

- *Who are you talking to?* In the play, who is the other person that you're talking to? What is your relationship to them? Choose someone from your real life that is similar to the relationship that your character has with the person that they're talking to. For instance, if the character that you're talking to is a captain in the army, and you've never been in the army, what do you do? Look at the *essence* of that relationship. You may have never been in the army, but at some point you've been subservient to a superior. Perhaps when you were a student and you went to the principal. There might be time as a child when you had a meeting with your priest or rabbi. The more specific and truthful you can be in personalizing who you're speaking to in your monologue, the more effective it will be. *Who the other person is and your ability to believably communicate with him or her is one of the keys to giving a successful monologue audition.*

COMMUNICATION WITH THE
OTHER CHARACTER

In life when you are communicating with another person, it's like there are imaginary arrows that carry your words and thoughts from yourself to that other person. These imaginary arrows communicate information and your intentions to that person. When these arrows hit, the communication has (hopefully) been received, and what you were trying to say has been understood by the other person. At this point in the communication, the other person responds in some way. It may be a verbal response: he might say something. Or it might just be a look in his eyes that let's you know "he got it." After you notice he has got it, you continue the conversation, going on to your next idea. How the other person responded, that look in his eyes when he got it, will flavor what you say next and quite often how you say it. This is how basic communications works.

Generally, this whole process occurs quite quickly, so we don't even notice or think about it. When we're communicating, the arrows go from us to the other person and back to us and back to him, and so on. There is an ongoing *circle of communication* between you and your listener. This is an important concept to understand when doing a monologue for an audition.

Your job when performing a monologue for an audition is to make the auditors believe that you are truly communicating with another person (even though no one is actually there). Most actors when rehearsing their monologue (and at the audition) generally pay little attention to the imaginary person that they're talking to. Perhaps they pick a spot on the back wall and talk to it. They've never really investigated what it would be like to actually say those words to a real person from their real lives. Adding that imaginary person, then attempting to communicate with him, imagining his response as you speak, then continuing until you're through speaking is what's required in the monologue audition.

The more you *need* to communicate to that imaginary person, the more effective and dynamic your monologue will be. Unless you give the impression that you're actually speaking to another person, there will always be a slight flatness in your performance, no matter how good an actor you are.

Most monologues are "duologues"; the other person just happens not to be saying anything at the time. This idea of the imaginary person is not very different than the job of the actor in a monster movie who has to react to the monster that's not really there. The movie actor is actually speaking to a blue screen; the monster will be added by computer at a later time.

I remember when watching the movie *Stuart Little*, I was so impressed how successfully the actors reacted to the little mouse who wasn't there. They had full conversations to an imaginary scene partner. This is similar to the job you have when working on your monologues.

Always try to place the imaginary character that you're speaking to out front, perhaps above the heads of the people you're auditioning for. I've seen actors place the imaginary person right next to them, say in a car scene, thereby giving the auditors their profile for the entire audition, not a good idea. The auditors want to see your eyes, your face, hear your voice. Don't cheat yourself by upstaging yourself during audition. Play toward the auditors. You have a couple of minutes; don't waste a second of it with your back to them.

I've seen actors put an empty chair where the other character is supposed to be sitting in the scene. They then start talking to the empty chair. Don't do that; it doesn't work and it looks silly.

You should place your imaginary other character either downstage center, downstage right, or downstage left. You'll want to keep them at eye level. I can't tell you how often I've seen actors talking to imaginary characters that seem to be less than two feet tall. Remember, we'll be watching your eyes. If you're looking down toward the floor, that's where we'll assume the other person is supposed to be.

TO SIT OR NOT TO SIT DURING
THE MONOLOGUE AUDITION

Most auditions provide a chair that the actor has the option of using during their audition. Please note I said the option of using. A great many actors use the chair even if the material that they are performing doesn't require them to be seated. Being seated makes actors feel grounded, safe, in control. I've seen actors do monologues where the character is totally out of control, having an emotional tirade, but the actor has chosen to remain seated for the entire audition.

What determines whether you should be seated or not? The answer quite simply is the material that you're auditioning. If the monologue takes place at a table in a restaurant where you're conversing with someone at the table, obviously you should be seated. If it's a high-energy, say, relationship-ending monologue, where one person is leaving his spouse, how can you stay in your seat? For some monologues, the character might start out being seated and then get up and move around.

When you first start out working on a new monologue, it's perfectly OK to be seated for the first table-reads. But as you progress, *if it feels natural,* get up, move about, try things. The only thing you don't want to do is upstage yourself while you are speaking. Make sure that the auditors at the audition can see you. Other than that, if it feels natural, get up and move around; trust your instincts.

I've recently heard that some casting directors no longer provide chairs at auditions. Aware that it's a crutch for many actors, they want to see how the actor deals without one. I personally feel that it is not reasonable or fair to insist that all monologues be performed standing, since many monologues are clearly meant to be delivered seated. If you find yourself auditioning for one of these casting directors, you will have to adjust the monologue to a standing delivery and be able to justify it. Prepare in advance by practicing a standing version of your monologue.

DEALING WITH THOSE
NEGATIVE VOICES IN YOUR HEAD

One thing my students constantly deal with is the self-critical voice that exists in all our minds. I'm talking about that nagging voice that all artists seem to have. There you are trying to rehearse your monologue, but in the back of your mind, a voice is saying, "That's not good enough. You're not talented. Too slow. Nobody will believe you." On and on it goes. That self-critical voice can sabotage your work and deplete your energy. It causes you to lose your concentration; it makes you miserable. The sad part is that voice may be with you for the rest of your life. I'm not a shrink, so I don't know how it got there. All I know is that almost all my students mention it at some point in their work. Artists deal with it all the time; they always have. That being the case, you must learn to come to terms with the self-critical voice and not let it throw you off track.

One exercise that I do with my students is to have them literally yell back at that self-critical voice in their head when it they lose their focus. I have them yell things like "Shut up, I'm working here!" "Keep quiet!" — or anything else that'll let the voice know that *you* are in charge. Then they immediately return to their work on the monologue. By always staying in the moment, staying fully concentrated on what you're saying in the monologue, you'll notice that the voice sometimes softens, perhaps even dwindles away.

BEING PRIVATE IN PUBLIC

Sometimes a student will tell me how wonderful his performance of a monologue was when he rehearsed it alone at home. He'll tell me how emotionally free he felt, how alive the piece was. In my studio, I always try to provide a safe, nonjudgmental space for actors to work in. But nothing, I realize, is as safe as your own room when you're alone. As a joke, I'll sometimes tell the actor that perhaps I should make house calls to see his wonderful monologue rehearsals. Acting is a performance art. You rehearse so that you can eventually perform your work before a live audience.

Some actors try to block out the auditors at an audition or an audience at a performance. I personally don't think that's the best way to deal with your fears. They (the auditors and the audience) are there, and rather than putting your energy (and concentration) into pretending that they're not there, focus on the world of the piece that you're performing. Acknowledge that they're there and stay focused and in the moment. Don't empower the casting directors to a point where they can distract you from your work.

SETTING IT TOO TIGHTLY

We've all experienced those auditions where we delivered the monologue *exactly* as we rehearsed it; I mean *exactly!* Every phrase, every movement, every moment performed just as we had worked on it at home. We left the audition room feeling somewhat successful because we did indeed hit every mark. But somewhere inside there was a feeling that perhaps we were too safe, maybe we were just too overrehearsed. We performed "too tightly."

Then there are those other auditions, where (perhaps by accident) we threw ourselves completely into the material, felt it wholeheartedly. The material went to a whole other place. Our work was more meaningful, richer, deeper, and, most of all, more *spontaneous*. We discovered something about the character and ourselves that we never knew existed.

At the end of those magical auditions, you don't want to leave the audition room; you want to stay there forever, hold on to the moment. The reason that you don't want to leave is because you've experienced why you really want to act in the first place. You "danced on the edge of the sword," and you loved it. You were private in public. These are the kinds of auditions you should strive for; the dangerous ones where anything can happen, and you're willing to fail.

PROPS

My feeling about props at auditions is that you should try at all costs to avoid them. I've seen actors bring an array of props and make their audition more about the props then their acting. Even in phone monologues, which in themselves can be tricky for auditions, you don't need to bring in a real phone. You can simply mime the phone. If you feel that your monologue must include a prop, try not to spend too much time dealing with it, just set it and forget it. Again, it's your acting the auditors want to see not how well you deal with props.

chapter 8

The Monologue Audition

WHAT CASTING DIRECTORS ARE LOOKING FOR

Believe it or not, they're looking for you — if you've got talent. The reason that they're sitting there for hours and hours is to find talented actors to fill roles that they're casting. Every time a talented actor comes in well prepared with a monologue that truly showcases them, it really excites them and makes their job more enjoyable. *They really want to like you!* Many actors have the neurotic notion that casting directors are somehow their enemy. Nothing could be further from the truth. They are your allies; you're all in this together.

You've got to remember that the monologue audition is a five-minute job interview. *Everything counts.* You're being judged not just on your talent but also on how and who you are. Attitude is a very important part of an audition. I've been at auditions where the actor gives a brilliant performance but doesn't have a clue about how to present himself. If an actor comes across as too needy or hostile or insecure, a red flag goes up.

Casting directors are looking for confident actors who enter with a sense of self and take charge of their auditions. They want to see actors who are both friendly and professional. You must give them the impression that you really want to be there. So many actors slither on the stage and look uncomfortable for the entire audition. You must give them the impression that the audition stage is as comfortable as your room at home.

Casting directors are looking for actors who come in prepared, who have made specific choices and have the ability to perform them spontaneously. Casting directors don't want actors who waste time in the audition room preparing.

Casting directors want an actor who is willing to expose his emotions. Quite often actors don't realize that their job is not only to feel the role but also to be willing to share their honest emotions with others. Nothing is more boring than the self-indulgent actor who is sitting up there immersed in his own feelings and not willing (or able) to communicate them to an audience.

The director is asking himself, *"Can I work with this person?"* The producer is asking himself, *"Can I bank on this person?"* The playwright is asking himself, *"Will this actor be able to perform the role?"* Everyone on the creative team has his own insecurities, his own agenda. Part of your job is to make them all feel that you're not going to be a problem for them in their production. You must come across as confident, accessible, and professional. They don't want to work with actors who put out a negative attitude. Would you?

TEN STEPS TO A SUCCESSFUL MONOLOGUE AUDITION

1. The first step begins before the actual audition. Before you leave home in the morning, try to get yourself in the right frame of mind. Relax, perhaps do some breathing and stretching. Many actors I know begin their day using visualization techniques to imagine what they would like to happen at the audition.

2. You should arrive at your auditions at least twenty minutes before your assigned time. You should be friendly and professional to the person who greets you. Even though you may feel nervous, try to remain calm. Don't waste valuable time chatting with other actors or socializing. Once you've settled down, go off in a corner somewhere and begin to relax again. It's always helpful to do a quick run-through of the piece(s). This can be done softly and shouldn't be performed all out; save that for the audition.

3. There are *two faces* that you must be able to show at every audition. The first face is on you when you enter the audition room; it's your professional face. This is the friendly, confident face that tells them that you are a capable and reliable actor. Smile directly at the people auditioning you and say hello. In some cases you might already know them; you may have auditioned for them in the past. If that's the case, generally they'll greet you by name. The attitude in those instances will be a bit less formal. But this is not a time to be too friendly. You should always be totally professional, even if you've auditioned for them a dozen times. I recommend rehearsing these opening audition moments at home. You should not approach the auditors and shake their hands unless they indicate that they want you to. Many casting directors feel uncomfortable when actors invade their space. If you have to hand them your picture and résumé, do it quickly and efficiently, and then immediately go to your playing area and prepare to perform your monologue.

4. You should never begin your monologue until you've arrived at your playing area and have announced where the monologue is from. When you get to your playing area say your name clearly and then the name of the play that your monologue is from. If the monologue is not from a play, state the source material as clearly as possible. There is no reason to give a description of where in the play the monologue takes place. You don't need to set up the scene. If you are per-

forming two monologues for the audition, I recommend introducing the two at the beginning. That way you can easily glide from one character right into the next without having to return to yourself (the actor).

Be careful about upward inflections at the ends of your sentences. Actors, sometimes feeling nervous, will end their sentences with an upward inflection, which makes their sentences sound like questions rather than statements. Make sure that there is a period at the end of every one of your sentences. If the auditors wish to engage you in conversation, you must be willing to talk with them. Most casting directors save conversations for after you perform.

5. Give yourself a moment, and then allow the *second face* to be revealed. If you've done your preparation well in the waiting area, this face will be just beneath the professional face that you entered with earlier. It is the face, the persona, the mask of your character in the first monologue. Many actors mistakenly enter the audition room "in character." If the character in your opening monologue happens to be demonic, angry, or crazy, and that's how you enter the audition room, you're not going to start off on the right foot. The casting director might not know you and assume that this is you, the actor. This idea of two faces takes a bit of getting use to, but it should be part of your rehearsal process for all auditions.

6. After you've given yourself one last moment (to be certain that you're centered and ready to begin), start your monologue. Take your time, don't rush, and *don't forget to breathe* during the audition. In an attempt to maintain control, many actors forget to breathe during auditions. Breathe fully, breathe life into your character.

7. When you've completed performing the monologue, if they've requested a second one, prepare to make the transition from the first character to the second. Make sure the transition is clean (and should be well rehearsed at home before the au-

dition). You'll want to complete the first monologue, hold the moment, and then by a slight body movement, perhaps a turning of the head, or perhaps by walking to a nearby spot, prepare to begin the next monologue. Once again, give yourself a moment before you begin. Take your time, don't rush, and breathe.

8. After you've finished the monologue, take a moment, then make eye contact with the auditors again, smile, and let them know that you're through. Don't just drop the character or the moment after performing. It's appropriate at this time to say thank you. Try not to look into their eyes for any kind of approval. Maintain your composure, self-esteem, and professionalism. This part of the audition may feel uncomfortable since you've just performed for them and may feel vulnerable.

9. If they wish to talk with you, be prepared to stay and talk. The reason that they might be asking you to stay is that you've given a good audition and they may want to know you a little better, perhaps to see if you're the right person for their play. They may ask you the "so what have you been up to lately" question. Prepare the answer to this question in advance and be ready to tell them a bit about yourself. Your demeanor should be relaxed, professional, and friendly.

10. When they've finished talking with you, tell them it was great meeting them and leave in a confident, unhurried, professional manner. Once you leave the room, the only thing left to do is to let go of that audition and move on to the next part of your day.

USING THE CASTING DIRECTOR OR AGENT

Never ask the agent or casting director at an audition if you can use them as your scene partner. Hopefully you've been rehearsing with an imaginary person and wouldn't need to use the casting director for your audition. The casting director's and agent's job is to evaluate you as an actor *not* to be your scene partner. By using them for your scene partner, you are leaving yourself very vulnerable. How you perceive them looking at you will influence how you perform your monologue. If they look away, if they decide to look down at your résumé and ignore you, if they have a look of boredom or disdain, your performance might be thrown off.

Sometimes an agent or casting director may request that you use him. This is especially true for auditors considering you for film or television work. At that time, even if you've rehearsed with an imaginary person, you must be willing to make the adjustment.

"SO WHAT HAVE YOU BEEN UP TO LATELY?"

Throughout your acting career you will constantly be asked at interviews and auditions: "So what have you been up to lately?" It's very important that you know in advance how you want to respond. Interested casting directors, agents, and directors ask this question of actors to get some sense of them. Your response shouldn't be more than a minute or a minute and a half. It should include all recent significant activity in the business. It should not include too much about your personal life — perhaps where you grew up, what school you went to. Your answer should be positive, upbeat, and confident. It should not be memorized even though all the information should be; your answer should be spontaneous and positive.

This is not the time to put down that director you hated working with in your last play. If you're putting down your last director to these new people, they may very well wonder if you'll bad-mouth them at your next interview. Not a negative word should be spoken while answering this question. Everyone wants to work with a winner, and your answer should imply confidence and professionalism.

Don't lie! There is nothing worse than being caught in a lie of any size during an interview or audition. It invalidates you as a potential candidate. Trust me, it's not worth it.

A FOCUSED AUDITION

When you're performing your monologue for an audition, everything you say and do is being observed. Where your eyes gaze as well as how you move (or don't) is all part of the performance. I've seen actors perform large chunks of their monologue while staring at the floor. Where you focus your gaze and energy is a very important part of what they see. If you spend a lot of your audition staring at the floor, much of your good work will be buried.

Focusing your performance also applies to being heard. One of the first things you must immediately assess as you walk into the room is the acoustics. No matter what size the audition room or theater is, make sure your volume level is appropriate. You don't want to overwhelm them by yelling or make them strain to hear you by talking too softly. If you're auditioning in an agent's office, make sure your voice (and the material that you've selected) is appropriate. Remember, this is a workplace; you don't want to select material that has you yelling and jumping up and down.

Some actors glue their eyes to the imaginary person in their scene. They stare nonstop for the entire audition. This doesn't look realistic. Think of how you are in life. Very rarely will you lock eyes with someone you're talking to for an entire two minutes, even if it's an intense conversation. For a moment here or there, you'll look away, perhaps to gather your thoughts, notice something, or break the tension. Remember, when you're dealing with imaginary characters in your monologues, they will react to things that you're saying to them. The way that they react will affect how you say what you say and how and when you'll look at them.

Be sensitive to wasting the auditors' time at the audition. It's not professional to chat up the auditors before or after your monologue. Some actors mistakenly believe that by ingratiating themselves, by shmoozing, they'll somehow win brownie points. Actually, the opposite is true. The auditors have a lot of work to do in a very short period of time. The actor who monopolizes them in conversation wastes their time; time that they could be using to audition other actors. Be considerate; be succinct. Don't overstay your welcome; always leave them wanting more.

Try not to work too hard. Try to enjoy the experience of the audition. Relax, enjoy, and never let 'em see you sweat.

DEALING WITH THOSE ACTOR NERVES

Believe it or not, being nervous before an audition is a good thing. There is an energy to nerves that if utilized well can be very exciting. Harnessing your nervous energy should be part of your preparation. Brando supposedly did push-ups every night before going out on stage to perform. Some actors run in place before going on, while others sit and breathe deeply to focus their nerves. I always recommend that actors go off in a corner and do their monologue a few times before the actual audition. At first say the words softly, and then, if possible and appropriate do it at full voice. But don't do it full out, save that for the audition.

The most important thing about nerves is that you come to terms with them. More than likely they'll be there before almost every audition. Welcome them with open arms and find ways to make them your best friend.

WHEN YOU FEEL YOU'VE BLOWN IT

If you go up on your lines or make any mistakes during the audition, try to keep going. What might seem like a monumental mistake to you, might appear as barely a bleep on the auditors' radar screen. Complete the monologue and try to maintain your composure. I like to use the example of professional ice skaters who sometimes take bad falls during competitions. They immediately get up and continue their routine as if nothing had happened. At the end of their routine, they smile graciously and pretend that their fall to the ice was inconsequential. They may feel horrible inside, but they keep up the performance till after they have left the ice.

KEEPING YOUR MONOLOGUE FRESH

The more often you perform your monologue, the more difficult it will be to keep it fresh. Many actors go from audition to audition performing the same monologues on automatic pilot. There is nothing more boring for both you and the auditors than to perform and see material that's lost its spontaneity, its aliveness. Actors shortchange themselves by showing the results of what they previously discovered. You must go to every audition and be willing to start from scratch.

When discussing how he did eight performances a week in the lead role of Hamlet and kept it fresh, Kevin Kline is attributed to have said, "I know the first line; the rest is an improvisation." Whether he actually said that or not, the idea is valid for your monologue auditions. Rather than trying to play it safe and creating shortcuts, you must be willing to go to each and every audition and perform your monologue as if this was the first time. If you can no longer do that, if the material has become stale, drop it. There's a million monologues out there; find yourself some new ones.

WHAT TO WEAR TO YOUR AUDITION

Always dress neatly for all your auditions. You don't want to wear those funky clothes that you wear when hanging out with your friends (unless it is totally appropriate for a role that you're auditioning for).

Remember, this is a job interview. I do feel that you should wear clothing that somehow suggests the character that you're portraying in your monologue. If you're performing two monologues, your wardrobe choice will be a bit more difficult. Try to find something that somehow expresses both your characters. The wardrobe will probably have to be a bit more neutral. *Don't costume yourself for your monologue.* All you want to do is suggest the character. I've seen actors go to extremes in wardrobing themselves; it's not necessary or appropriate. You don't want to wear any clothing that inhibits movement, or any jewelry that can be distracting during your audition.

You'll always want to look like your headshot. Your headshot, by the way, *should look like you, exactly like you, on a very good day.* Don't do a makeover that radically changes your look. If you no longer look like your headshot, then it's time to get a new one.

And for callbacks, it's always a good idea to try to wear what you wore to the initial audition. If those clothes are in the cleaners, try to wear similar clothes. It's not a good idea to change your look for the callback.

LYING ON YOUR RÉSUMÉ

Simply put, don't lie on your résumé. It's not a fib; it's a lie. Occasionally a casting director or director will ask you about something that you have on your résumé. This is a very small industry; you'd be amazed at who knows whom. If you've lied on your résumé, you'll know it and will always be living with the fear that you'll be caught. There's nothing worse than giving a great audition and then being caught in a lie on your résumé.

If you're a young, inexperienced actor, it's not a great sin to not have much on your résumé. Don't feel that you need to impress people with fictitious credits. One way to fill an empty résumé is with classes, lots and lots of classes. Study with a variety of teachers and then list them on your résumé. Another popular way to fill a résumé is to get into some student and independent films. And don't forget to list those skills that you're good at (lift weights, run marathons, sail, speak four languages, and so on).

DEALING WITH DISCOURTEOUS CASTING DIRECTORS

Occasionally you'll audition for a casting director or agent who might be discourteous or unpleasant. Perhaps he's tired after sitting through too many auditions, or the actor right before you might have given him a hard time. Whatever the reason, all you know is that he's acting discourteously. Don't let it throw you. His bad behavior is *his* problem and most likely has nothing to do with you. You are there to audition; to show your work. The audition will be over in a few minutes. Remain professional, positive, and relaxed. The sign of a true professional is to carry on with dignity and grace. Be as a courteous as you can, perform better than you ever have, then smile, say thank you, and leave.

THE ENERGY THAT YOU BRING TO THE AUDITION

Sometimes actors are not aware of the emotional baggage that they bring into the audition room. An actor with a chip on his shoulder will rarely succeed, no matter how well he performs his monologue. The actor whose body language and personality express intense neediness will at best get the auditors sympathy, not a callback. And the actor entering with manic energy masquerading as confidence will only alienate the auditors who can see right through him. If you've spent your time before the audition relaxing, visualizing, and properly preparing, you'll realize that entering just as yourself is all you need to do.

PRACTICING RUN-THROUGHS OF YOUR MONOLOGUE AUDITION

One of the ways I help actors deal with the fear of auditioning is to have mock run-throughs of their monologue auditions. We rehearse the entire audition from entrance to exit. Usually I'll play a variety of casting director types; everything from the nice-guy casting director to the rudest one you'd never want to meet. The actor gets to experience different scenarios. You might want to try this exercise with another actor playing the different roles of the casting directors. You'll soon discover that there are only so many ways it can all turn out. And remember, generally monologue auditions are only five or ten minutes long. No matter how stressed out you are about it, it'll all be over before you know it. Rather than let it freak you out, see if you can actually go into that audition room and *enjoy* yourself.

chapter 9

Preparing for the General Interview

The general interview is a meeting with a casting director or agent. It's an opportunity for that person to get to know you. Generally, you'll be asked to perform one or two monologues for the interview. How well you perform the monologues is an important step toward an ongoing relationship with the casting director or agent.

You'll discover that the office interview is not always the best place to perform your monologue. The office may be small, and you may have to perform your piece seated directly across the desk from the agent. There is also all the office noise in the background to contend with; phones ringing, people talking, and so on.

Find out as much as you can about the person you're going to meet. If it's an agent, try to find out who some of the agency's clients are, how long the agency has been in the business, what type of reputation it has, if it has offices on both coasts, what it's franchised in (theater, television, film, commercials) — everything.

If it's a casting director, find out what he's cast in the past, what he's presently casting, and what he's slated to cast in the future. Find out how long the office has been in existence. Does it have offices on both coasts? What type of reputation does it have? Again, research, network, and call your friends. The more you can find out about the person who will be interviewing you, the more comfortable you'll feel. That knowledge will be helpful in alleviating your fears.

Once you have all the information you can find, the next step is to imagine the situation. When you think about it, most interviews, no matter what they're about, have a certain commonality. They begin when you enter the door; you say hello, you sit down, you talk, you do a monologue or two, and then you say good-bye. That's about all that's going to happen. There shouldn't be too many other surprises.

While at home, improvise what you'll say. I use the word *improvise* because the last thing you want is to sound like some kind of machine spewing out memorized facts and information about yourself. Don't rehearse a memorized script; improvise and remain loose.

You can be assured that interviewers will ask certain basic questions such as: "So what have you been up to? Tell me about yourself." After looking at your résumé for a moment, they may start chatting with you about a theater that you've mentioned or a director they're familiar with. This is not a quiz! Don't get uptight. Prepare in advance by being very familiar with everything on your résumé. While improvising at home, create imaginary conversations about items on your résumé. Try to be positive in everything that you say. Even in the case of those horrible professional experiences that you may have had, give them a positive spin. Nobody wants to hear an actor whining or complaining at an interview.

One of the great benefits of doing all this preparation before the interview is the feeling of confidence you'll have when you actually go in for the interview. You know that you've prepared to the best of your ability. And even though you still may be nervous, you'll be a lot more confident.

SUCCESSFUL INTERVIEW TECHNIQUE

A talent agent's time is valuable. When you are asked to tell something about yourself, make your answer concise, interesting, personal, and to the point. He isn't interested in your personal life, but he is interested in your professional life. I know that sometimes these areas seem to blend, and that's where problems can come in. Always keep your interview with the agent professional. You can be cordial and friendly, but always maintain a professional demeanor. Some questions that might be going through his mind are:

- Will I be able to get this actor work?
- Do I get calls for his type?
- I wonder what his range is?
- What types of roles would he be right for?
- How would he do in film, television, on daytime serials?
- Does he have enough training or should I suggest some coaches or schools to him?
- Will I feel comfortable working with him, or will he be a problem?
- Will he be reliable, show up at auditions, and be professional?
- How serious is he about his career?
- Is he shopping around with many other agents?
- Is everything on his résumé truthful?
- Is there anything in his past that I should know about?

Confidence is crucial in the interview. You must muster up all the confidence you can *before* you walk in that door. How you present yourself is very important. You can't just wing it when you walk in. Work on yourself, prepare, get yourself psyched. Be totally prepared before you walk in that door. Be prepared to give clear, intelligent responses to the following questions:

- Why are you interested in show business?
- What does your career mean to you?
- Why would this agency be right for you and your needs as an actor?
- What are your career goals?
- Do you plan on living just in New York or are you thinking of being bicoastal?
- Where do you primarily want to focus — film, theater, or television?
- Besides your career, what other things do you do?
- Have you worked with other agents before? Have you ever been signed before?
- What kind of things have you been doing on your own for your career?

Prepare a loose script of answers to all these questions. Don't memorize your answers, but be ready to call upon the information in an impromptu manner.

YUP, HERE IT IS AGAIN: "SO WHAT HAVE YOU BEEN DOING LATELY?"

Here's that question again that you're almost always guaranteed to be asked at almost every interview. Your answer, as I've mentioned previously, must be prepared well in advance. Again, you don't want to recite a memorized script, but the information should be at your fingertips. How you deliver your answer is almost as important as what you've got to say. Your demeanor is paramount. There is a thin line between arrogance and confidence. Underlying arrogance usually indicates insecurity. Agents are aware of this. You must come from as positive a place as possible when being interviewed. You must seem genuinely enthusiastic about your future. This is not the time for shyness, hoping that the interviewer will draw you out. Make his job easy, not a task. Be forthcoming and have a smile that emanates from inside as well as on your face. Be proud of yourself and let that come across.

Much of the information that you'll be discussing will already be on your résumé. Be sure to bring to the interviewer's attention to anything of importance that you've done that might not be there. If you've been a day player on one of the daytime serials recently, let him know. If you've just had a callback for a play or movie and are still waiting to hear from them, let him know. Any positive recent activity (callbacks, interviews) that you think will be of interest to him, let him know and give it a positive spin. Once again, accentuate only the positive during this interview. Attitude is everything, especially if you don't have a great deal of work under your belt. He doesn't care about the problems in your life. He's not your father, shrink, or best friend. The agent wants to see potential, possibility, and a successful career in your future.

chapter 10

Interviews with Casting Directors

JAMES CALLERI, PLAYWRIGHTS HORIZONS

James Calleri is the casting director for Playwrights Horizons in New York City. He also cast the NBC television show "Ed and Monk." heater highlights include James Joyce's *The Dead* (Broadway and National Tour), Chris Durang's *Betty's Summer Vacation*, Richard Nelson's *Goodnight Children Everywhere* and *Franny's Vacation*, and Kenneth Lonergan's *Lobby Hero*. Other credits include: *Fully Committed* (NY and LA), *The Vagina Monologues* (National Tour), *The Syringa Tree*, and *The Guys*. Regional credits include The Mark Taper Forum, ACT, Goodman, Huntington, Seattle Rep, Alley, and Globe. Member of Casting Society of America. Twice awarded the Artios Award for Outstanding Achievement in Casting.

ALAN FILDERMAN

Alan Filderman's casting credits include: *Marie Christine, Master Class, Once on This Island, Miss Evers Boys, A New Brain, Three Tall Women, Song of Singapore,* and *The Sum of Us* (Broadway, Off Broadway, and National Tour). Regional credits include: Syracuse Stage, The Philadelphia Theatre Company, Berkshire Theatre Festival, and many others. Other credits include the films *Ice Age* and *Anastasia* and "Out of the Box" on television. Member of Casting Society of America.

CHARLES ROSEN

Clio Award–winner Charles Rosen is a graduate of Emerson College and has an extensive background in the performing arts. He began as an agent for the Fifi Oscard Agency in 1975. By 1988 he had successfully cast for major ad agencies such as Compton and Ogilvy and Mather. Charles became an independent casting director in 1989 and has been casting films, television, radio commercials, print campaigns, voice-overs, industrials, staged readings, workshops, and New York and regional theaters ever since.

DIANE HEERY, MIKE LEMON CASTING

Diane Heery started in the business as an actor. Having performed in all media, she can understand what an actor is going through. For the past ten years, she has been a casting director, working on projects such as *The Sixth Sense* and *Jersey Girl.* She is currently working on the CBS-TV series "Hack."

The Mike Lemon Casting office is open and friendly. People there consider it their job to make actors feel comfortable and welcome so that they can give their best during the audition. The office has a monthly open-call for talent; actors need to preregister. Information about the open calls can be found on their Web site: www.mikelemoncasting.com. They attend live theater/ showcases at least once a week.

ARNOLD MUNGIOLI,
MUNGIOLI THEATRICALS, INC.

Mungioli Theatricals, Inc. has cast for *Aladdin* for Disney Entertainment and *When You Wish* for Disney Theatrical Productions, as well as Richard Maltby's *The Sixties Project* and Stephen Schwartz's *Captain Louie.* Other projects include *Annie, The Long Christmas Ride Home, Homebody/Kabul,* and *Peter Pan* for Trinity Repertory Company; *Pacific Overtures* and *As You Like It* for the Chicago Shakespeare Theatre; and *Damn Yankees* at Chicago's Marriott Lincolnshire Theatre. President Arnold J. Mungioli, former executive director of Disney Theatrical Productions, has also cast the Broadway and international premieres of four companies of *Ragtime,* two companies of *Fosse,* five companies of the Hal Prince/Susan Stroman production of *Showboat, Candide, Music of the Night, Sunset Boulevard, Kiss of the Spiderwoman, Joseph and the Amazing Technicolor Dream Coat,* and many other productions, including the initial workshop productions of *Seussical* and *Sweet Smell of Success.* Mungioli has received two Artios Awards from the Casting Society of America for outstanding achievement. As a director, he has worked at MCC Theatre, the John Houseman Theatre, Provincetown Theatre Company, National Shakespeare Conservatory, and others. Mungioli currently serves on the adjunct faculty of the Tisch School of the Arts of New York University and has worked internationally, teaching master classes and seminars in New York, Los Angeles, and Toronto and has cast throughout North America, Europe, Africa, Asia, and Australia. Mungioli says of acting, "I love actors! In the words of Larry Kert to Donna McKechnie, as he lay dying, 'You know. It's noble what we do.' I truly believe that!" Find out more on their Web site: www.mungioli theatricals.com.

BREANNA BENJAMIN

After graduating from the University of Nebraska, Breanna Benjamin began a four-year stint as Miss Ann, the teacher on the CBS syndicated television series "Romper Room." Using her knowledge and affinity for working with talent, coupled with her desire to work behind the scenes, Benjamin founded a talent management company. As a casting director, her casting credits include motions picture festival award winners, commercial Cleo Award winners, and theater award honorees. Benjamin is credited with launching the careers of many fine actors, including Ally Sheedy, Peter Reckell, Tom Sizemore, Ron Eldard, Kyle Secor, and Amanda Bearse.

Benjamin has produced a pilot for the ABC television network, a dramatic special for PBS, and telethons and pageants, both local and televised. She also produced a series of two hundred reading tapes for educational use, sponsored by General Electric. Benjamin served as creative consultant on Scholastic Sports Academy Soccer Series for USA Cable Network.

Benjamin has been listed in *Who's Who in Theatre* and *Who's Who in Business Executives.* She has been a member of New York Women in Film and Television and was past president of Midwest Broadway Theatre League. She has been on the Blue Ribbon Panel for the Emmy Awards and is a Cable Ace Award Winner.

ADRIENNE STERN

Adrienne Stern casts for both theater and film. Her films have appeared at Sundance, Toronto, Berlin, Venice, and Seattle, and many have won prestigious awards. In 2002, she had five films out in the theaters: *The Believer* (Sundance Grand Jury Award), *Thirteen Conversations About One Thing, Snipes, The Next Big Thing,* and *Never Again.* In 2003, she cast for the film *On-Line*, starring Harrold Perrineau and Josh Hamilton. Stern is a member of BAFTA, New York Women in Film, and the Ensemble Studio Theater. She says about casting, "The casting of a play or film is the most essential element that goes into a project. As a casting director for the last thirteen years, the greatest gift is giving a performer the opportunity to use her craft."

INTERVIEWS

1. What is the first thing you look for when an actor enters the audition room (your office, the theater) to audition for you?

CALLERI: An interesting, fascinating person.

FILDERMAN: A professional but still open demeanor.

ROSEN: Confidence.

HEERY: It's important that an actor *looks* prepared — picture/résumé already out of the briefcase, coat off, etc. The talent's overall attitude of preparedness and confidence comes across right away.

MUNGIOLI: Confidence. I want to see someone who walks in the room having done his homework and is ready to work. I want to see a person who has been busy keeping himself in a positive mind-set with affirmations work and gratitude journals and belief in the great world of this work. Not someone who has been beaten up by this business and is dragging all of that baggage and a chip on his shoulder into the audition room with him!

BENJAMIN: Often I can tell before a person gets to my desk or the audition table if he or she is going to have a chance at booking the job — their confidence, personal appearance, how they introduce themselves. Some actors feel they have to make an entrance. That's just not so. Be yourself. Over the top does not work. A broken hand from a handshake doesn't work. Just come in as the best possible self. Dress neat and clean, put together, friendly, knowing that we want you there and are happy to see you. We see an average of thirty actors for a role; we have thousands to choose from. Obviously we think you are pretty right for the job or we wouldn't have invited you. That's even the same for open calls. Just believe in yourself. Don't let your personality overshadow your character/audition.

STERN: I look at how they carry themselves, speak, and their whole demeanor. How comfortable they are.

2. What do you feel are the most common mistakes actors make at their monologue auditions or at any audition?

CALLERI: A common mistake is addressing the auditor with the monologue: It makes me feel like I need to be there for the actor, and yet I'm really trying to evaluate and work. Most pieces are too long. It should be done in about a minute, minute and a half tops. After that, I get bored and want to move on.

FILDERMAN: A. Doing monologues that are not right for them (i.e., a woman in her early twenties doing Blanche). B. Doing a monologue that is so out there that the auditor spends all his time and energy trying to figure out what the hell the monologue is about. C. Doing a monologue that is either too short or too long — both are mistakes. Two minutes is just about right. D. Doing a monologue without having read the *entire* play that the monologue is from. E. Taking a scene and removing the other character and calling it a monologue.

ROSEN: Feeling nervous and not prepared.

HEERY : Many times, actors get too involved in themselves and don't *listen* to direction! Being nervous is OK at an audition, but you must stay conscious of the world around you. Many times the director asks an actor to alter something, then the actor just repeats his rehearsed piece without fully incorporating the direction in the retake.

MUNGIOLI: The most common mistake is actors failing to make an active choice with their monologues. Most commonly they choose some version of "to tell," that is "to let the person

I am speaking to know this or that . . ." or "to explain to the person I am speaking to . . ." It is invariably a weak choice and gives them no support in the audition. The second most common mistake is talking to the auditors at the table about the piece the actor is doing. In my experience, the actors who get the job do not do this.

BENJAMIN: They don't listen to the director or casting director. Listening is key. Often the actor is so busy thinking of what to do or say next to impress us that he doesn't listen to what we are telling him. Then he does or asks to do what has already been told to him not to do. Another big mistake is preparing in front of the auditors. We don't want to see you take a moment to exercise or deep breathe or meditate. Just do your audition material. I'm quite certain that when your film, television, or theater director says action, you're not going to be able to "take a moment."

STERN: Telling you what their monologue is about or who wrote it; forgetting their lines halfway through and not knowing how to fake it; choosing to do an accent when one has not been asked for.

3. What types of material do you suggest actors avoid selecting for monologue auditions? Why?

CALLERI: Avoid picking things that run the gamut from A to Z. No one can do that in a minute. I just want something that is close to the person (age and type). Avoid high emotion. Nine times out of ten, girls cry; boys scream and shout.

FILDERMAN: Avoid monologues that are not from plays and just exist in themselves. There is no character to play, no history to bring to the monologue. Avoid doing anything too violent or upsetting; ask yourself if the auditor would want to sit through this piece.

ROSEN: Poorly delivered heavy drama. It's embarrassing.

HEERY : Memory pieces are the least interesting to me. Seeing an actor recall a past emotional incident works in the com-

plete production of the play, but when played as a monologue, many times can look to me like a therapy session. A
third-person monologue never works for me — same goes
for poems, lawyer summations, anything from *Spoon River
Anthology,* or the Gettysburg Address. Also, a piece that is
obscene or vulgar just for the shock value accomplishes nothing; and no one enjoys being lectured or yelled at.

MUNGIOLI: Avoid material that is not age-appropriate. It is always best to present yourself with material from roles in
which you could realistically be cast! Be imaginative in your
choice of material, but do not be ridiculous and out of touch.

BENJAMIN: Avoid choosing the most popular pieces. If it's something that a superstar is known for, we're going to compare
you and we have preconceived ideas. It's going to be nearly
impossible for you to measure up. Don't pick something for
which you are absolutely the wrong physical type. It does-
n't matter if you "just like it"; it won't work.

STERN: Anything currently running or something so famous that
all you think about is the well-known actor that actually got
to say those words; anything with an accent — we can't tell
who you are. Anything you wrote yourself — it may work
against you if the auditor has to try and figure out where
the monologue comes from. And absolutely no props ever.

4. What types of material do you recommend? Why?

CALLERI: Simple pieces. I recommend knowing who you are auditioning for. Know the type of work we do. I cast for a theater that does new American writers. So seeing Goneril from
Lear would probably not be a good idea.

FILDERMAN: An actor should look for a piece that is close to
who he or she is, that he or she can relate to.

ROSEN: Comedy, I enjoy being entertained.

HEERY : I think that the most interesting monologues are "active" pieces; something that is happening right now to the
actor. I know that they are the most difficult to find, but when

that active monologue shows up on a full day of audition-ing talent, it certainly stands out! The piece should have at least three transitions in it and be *age-appropriate*.

MUNGIOLI: I recommend material that the actor emotionally connects with — material that speaks to what the actor, him-or herself, has to say. One way to do this is by finding an author you can connect with. Then, read every play you can get your hands on that that author has written, and you will likely find a monologue with which you connect.

BENJAMIN: Pick something that is type- and age-appropriate, a piece that goes somewhere and has something to say, not just a little slice-of-life piece — boring. Show some emotion. Pick a piece that you might actually be cast to perform.

STERN: A short story with a beginning, middle, and end, some-thing with a punch line that may make you laugh.

5. Particularly what things do you personally look for during the monologue audition?

CALLERI: I see it as getting to know the actor. I equate it to a first date. No one gets cast from doing a monologue. You move to the next step, though — an audition or meeting on a more specific project.

FILDERMAN: Speech skills, a comfortable body language, an emo-tional connection to the text.

ROSEN: An actor's ability to go with the choice/choices.

HEERY : I look for an actor who makes me forget that I'm watch-ing an audition! The actor should be fully involved in his or her character without projecting that he or she is conscious of being watched.

MUNGIOLI: An actor who has done his or her homework and made choices that are bold yet logical. An actor who is con-fident — not afraid of doing a monologue or annoyed by the request. An actor who has made an *active* choice and is using the words he or she is speaking to play an action — not just narrating a story or telling us something; an actor who does monologues as part of his or her trade and enjoys that work — not an actor who had to go out and pick a monologue to do and memorize it and work it up in the time since he or she got the appointment.

BENJAMIN: Is the actor the character? Has he or she checked out of the physical surroundings and gotten into the world of the character?

STERN: Speech patterns, character development, ease and flow with diction, complete awareness of their surroundings, comfortable body language.

6. What do actors do at auditions that upset or annoy you, and do you have any suggestions how they might remedy them?

CALLERI: See my answer for question number 7.

FILDERMAN: Being late, being unprepared, chatting too much, asking too many questions, being defensive, having an attitude.

ROSEN: Make excuses as to why they are not prepared.

HEERY : Be prepared! Be sure that your audition is not only memorized, but at performance level! Remember that this is the casting director's first impression of you. You want to be remembered for your talent, not because you weren't ready. In my humble opinion, a monologue is something that you have lived with for a while; you have rehearsed it, performed it for someone, and received critiques on it. Please don't insult the auditors by bringing a piece that you just learned the day before. You want to present yourself as prepared, polished, and professional. One peeve: Be on time! Your appointment time means the time you *enter the studio* — not your arrival time.

MUNGIOLI: An actor who is not prepared and flexible can be a burden to the audition process. If you have been asked to prepare one kind of monologue (say, a contemporary classic piece) and in the course of the audition you are asked if you have a classical dramatic piece, do not give excuses about not having been asked to prepare it in advance. *Sempere parare!* Be flexible! We may be thinking of you for a different part in the show — or even a larger part in a different show we are working on. Be cheerful! Be prepared!

BENJAMIN: Have you noticed how many actors slap themselves? I mean that. Their nerves somehow entice them to keep slapping their thighs to emphasize words. This only shows us that they are nervous. Please listen to the director. Do what the director asks in the way of directing the piece, even if you think it's wrong. Don't argue or defend your choice. Maybe the director is also thinking of another project he or she is doing and just wants to see if you can make the adjustment. Do your audition, thank the auditors, and leave us remembering your audition. Don't try and start a big conversation or try to be witty; we want to remember your acting.

STERN: Please when it is over and they thank you, walk out of the room. Do not stand there putting your coat on. This is our short period between actors to talk or regroup. And never ask, "When will I hear from you?"

7. In general, any advice for actors regarding monologue auditions?

CALLERI: See my reply to questions 6 and 7. Most monologues are too long; always leave us wanting more. Make sure the other person in the piece, although he or she is not present in the room, is clear and vivid for you. Your performance is all about responding to the reactions from the other imaginary person. Those reactions and responses from the imaginary partner must be strong and specific; this is what propels you to keep speaking.

FILDERMAN: Be on time, be prepared, and be good.

ROSEN: Your job is to entertain. Choose material that you can commit to.

HEERY : Actors should remember that just the *choice* of monologue tells a lot about how you perceive yourself and how you present your talent to others. No one forced you to use that particular piece; it should be something that speaks to you.

MUNGIOLI: See my reply to question number 6. And dress presentably! This is a profession; be professional.

BENJAMIN: Know your stuff, deliver it, and say good-bye. We'll thank you for it.

STERN: Try to avoid them at all costs.

chapter 11

Interviews with Talent Agents

JERRY HOGAN,
HENDERSON HOGAN TALENT AGENCY

Originally Jerry Hogan was an actor. He began in musical theater. Finding the instability of being an actor not for him, he
became private secretary to actress Margaret Leighton before
moving to the Dudley, Field and Malone Agency. Hogan worked
as a commercial agent at United Talent, before joining Margaret
Henderson while she was still partnered with Joan Scott at the
Henderson Scott Agency.

The Henderson Hogan Talent Agency looks for actors who
are intelligent and trained. Agents also look for actors who have
charisma and are able to communicate and keep the conversation going during the agency interview. Sometimes a "look"
gives agents an incentive to call an actor, "[b]ut then it has to
be followed up by diligence and determination to work hard."
The agency has found clients through theater schools, submissions, and referrals.

MICHAEL KIRSTEN,
HARDEN-CURTIS ASSOCIATES

Michael Kirsten has been an agent at Harden-Curtis Associates for six years. He has been performing in and studying theater since his childhood. Kirsten studied theater performance at Northwestern University, where he earned a bachelor's degree in communication, with a major in theater. Kirsten worked for four years as an actor, primarily in regional theaters throughout the country. He has experienced this business from both sides of the table.

B. LYNNE JEBBINS, THE KRASNY OFFICE

B. Lynne Jebbins received a BFA in theater from Illinois Wesleyan University. She then did graduate work in directing and acting at the University of Georgia, studying with Leighton Ballew, who was one of the top directing teachers in the country. She decided to learn the business end of the entertainment industry and began working at an agency. She says about acting and being an agent, "I say this with great love and respect, but I think it takes a special kind of . . . naïveté or stubbornness or strength to survive being an actor. I didn't know if it was there for me anymore, so I stayed with being an agent. I have enjoyed agenting. I am still dealing with the people who drew me into acting — the actors! They are fascinating, incredible people, even if I do want to put a few of them out of their misery at times!"

BARRY KOLKER, THE CARSON ORGANIZATION

Barry Kolker began as an actor but gave it up over thirteen years ago. He has been a talent agent for eleven years, representing children and adults. Kolker says of himself, "I consider myself 24/7/365, trying to get my clients work in theater, film, and television. I have even been reached on vacations and negotiated deals on New Year's Eve and during the Tony Awards!"

INTERVIEWS

1. What is the first thing you look for when an actor enters the audition room — your office or the theater — to audition for you?

HOGAN: Their ability to command the stage, to take the stage and just do it. Always come in and just begin to do the material unless asked to speak. Do it with assurance!

KIRSTEN: The résumé is very important to me. I want to see that actors have trained and been in class, whether at a university or in conservatory. Without training and technique, you cannot master the craft. I also look for how the actor is presenting himself. Is he dressed appropriately? Is he confident? Is he overeager?

JEBBINS: One of the first things I look for in an actor is a quiet confidence. I want someone who is a nice person. I try to make the actors comfortable, and, boy, if they can't be comfortable around me, they are not going to be around anyone in this business. I want them to present themselves in a positive way because they will also be representing the agency.

KOLKER: An actor or actress should be neat and professionally dressed and prepared to do a monologue. If you don't know what to prepare, ask the receptionist or assistant, when you are making your appointment on the phone, what is expected of you.

2. What do you feel are the most common mistakes actors make at their monologue auditions or at any audition?

HOGAN : Apologizing for the material or the quality or their lack of preparation before or after the audition. Do not talk too much unless asked a question. Overall, if you make a mistake, make it big.

KIRSTEN : You must make a choice. Whether it's a good choice or bad choice will be up to the auditor, but being passive will have you lost in the shuffle. You need to be grounded. Don't wander around the playing area. Unnecessary movement weakens what you are saying. And choose a strong focus point. Know whom you are talking to.

JEBBINS: I think two of the most common mistakes actors make are picking material that is not right for them, and I truly believe it wrong to do movie and film scripts. I know that there are a lot of teachers today who are telling actors to do movie scripts. But I don't think that is fair to the actor. It means that they have to compete with a two-story-high celluloid memory, and in this day and age of VCRs, we can watch movies fifty times. You are never going to know if that is the favorite of the persons you are auditioning for — so why take the chance!

KOLKER : I have had actors look away, at the wall or to a place where I couldn't see their face. Monologues that go on too long (more than five minutes). I have had actors unprepared to perform anything.

3. What types of material do you suggest actors avoid selecting for monologue auditions? Why?

HOGAN: Wordy or complicated material. Material that doesn't fit your type. Simplify and make specific choices for your material. If you're not right for the role, don't assume you could be by your reading. They want what you can bring to a role that is unique from another actor's choices.

KIRSTEN : Avoid film and television monologues. The writing is often not as good. And, particularly with film, many times you are competing against an image that is embedded in our heads. If I have seen Al Pacino in *The Godfather,* you are not going to top him. Instead, I'll be comparing you to his performance. And you'll lose every time.

JEBBINS : I realize that I am not the norm in this thinking, and I know that others in the business give actors a list of monologues they shouldn't do because they are overdone. But I feel that is just selfish on our end. Our job is to watch the actor do the work and not judge the piece on whether we like it or not. I don't believe in taking monologues from those monologue books. And don't do something and not have read the whole play! Big mistake!

KOLKER : Avoid classical unless you can really do it. Do not go beyond two minutes. Show personality; please don't bore us.

4. What types of material do you recommend? Why?

HOGAN : Effective material that you are comfortable with and are confident that you can do well. Follow through with a definite interpretation of the material.

KIRSTEN : Choose monologues that have an arc. And know what the arc is: Don't start the monologue at the top so you have nowhere to go. A monologue is a two-minute story with a beginning, middle, and end. Show all those parts. Know what you are auditioning for. Don't do a Chekhov monologue for a Neil Simon play. If it's a general audition and you have a choice, a lighter piece is usually better. We get tired of people yelling and crying all day.

JEBBINS : When you are picking material, pick something that makes you feel something. If it is not special to you, you won't make it special to us.

KOLKER : I prefer contemporary comedic to show personality. Avoid monologues about death. I was at a monologue workshop, and every third monologue was about death; it was too emotional.

5. Particularly what things do you personally look for during the monologue audition?

HOGAN : Ease of getting into material. Assured vocal presentation considering the size of the space.

KIRSTEN : All of the things I mentioned before — making choices, strong technique, keeping a good focus. Your choice of material is very important. Choose material that you are castable in. The time for stretching and playing a wide age range is over. Know who you are and what you do well and play to your strengths.

JEBBINS : I look for actors who can transform; ones who I can't see acting.

KOLKER : Personality and energy and a commitment and believability to the material.

6. What do actors do at auditions that upset or annoy you, and do you have any suggestions how they might remedy them?

HOGAN : Choosing material out of your range, unrehearsed material, and/or apologizing for your presentation. Keep your body language in check. *Practice! Practice! Practice!*

KIRSTEN : Never apologize. Ever. Be confident in what you do and stand by your performance. Don't roll your eyes because you thought you flopped. We don't want to see it. Don't come across as overeager. You are there to do a job. Walk in with confidence, blow us away with your performance, and then say good-bye. If one of the auditors wants to see more or chat, he will let you know.

JEBBINS : One of the biggest issues I have with actors and their monologues is that if you are supposed to be bringing in *contrasting* pieces, that's what I want to see. The bigger the contrast the more you will show me what you are capable of doing. Too many people pick two pieces that have characters that are just about the same.

KOLKER : Come prepared and know the lines. Do not pick a monologue that you just learned. Try it out on your teacher, coach, manager, family, or friends for their opinions before you do it for us. Does it work or not?

7. In general, any advice for actors regarding monologue auditions?

HOGAN : Approach it with ease, assurance, and command of the language.

KIRSTEN : Know who you are and choose appropriate material. Be confident and secure with yourself. Be kind to everyone inside and outside the room (diva talk gets back to us). Most important, be prepared!

JEBBINS : An old friend of mine once said to me that he had finally figured it all out. Walk in, be pleasant, expect nothing in return, do the work, walk out, and let it go. It is over. Actors should set out to do a good audition, not to get a job. It is the history of good auditions that will continue to get you in doors. Too many actors want to walk in and talk. Just do the work!

KOLKER : Pick monologues: one dramatic and one comedic, both contemporary. Also have two classical, if you can do it. Show personality. Do them in two minutes or less.

There are some talent agencies that do not have actors perform monologues for their office auditions. One such agency is Silver, Massetti, Szatmary/ East, Ltd. This is Diane Busch's response to monologue auditions.

DIANE BUSCH, SILVER, MASSETTI & SZATMARY/EAST, LTD.

Dianne Busch has been an agent for twelve years and was a casting director before that. She is a senior agent at Silver, Massetti & Szatmary/East, Ltd. She says about the agency, "Our office does not ask actors we meet to audition. I do however see monologues at school presentations each spring. Here are a few things that appeal to me: uniqueness, humor, and spontaneity. Choosing material close to your type and age is important because I need to know how you fit in the casting going on right now. I can tell from a résumé what else you can do. Showing contrast, such as toughness in one and vulnerability in another, is also a very good idea, as long as you really are right for both roles. Things that bug me: to see an actor become overserious, or to see an actor be rude to his fellow actors."

Actors' First and Favorite Monologue Anecdotes

What follows are some stories by well-known actors about their first or favorite audition monologues. I'm sure that you'll be able to relate to some of their first audition jitters and insecurities.

GLENN CLOSE

I did one of Hecuba's speeches from *The Trojan Women* for my TCG final auditions. No one told me that it might not be a good idea to go up in front of all those representatives of all the top regional theaters in the country and do an eighty-year-old woman. I don't think they quite knew what to do with me. I do know one thing — you could hear a pin drop during my speech; so at least they listened. Those auditions lead to my first job with the New Phoenix Repertory Company and my Broadway debut in the fall of 1974.

GLENNE HEADLY

I wouldn't be able to pick out just one favorite monologue because even in the days when I had to audition with monologues I didn't just have just one. I used to alternate between two. They were St. Joan conveying to the court what she saw when she went into a trance, from Anouillh's *The Lark,* and one from Sam Shepard, the title of which, believe it or not, I have now forgotten, where the character describes the beauty and excitement of fireworks lighting up the sky.

I found that whenever I had to audition for something serious or sad, the piece from *The Lark* worked very well. It was a gentle piece, and as the character got quite lost in her remembrance, so would I, thereby keeping my mind off the people I was auditioning for; who were always terrifying to me no matter how large or small the production.

When I was auditioning for a lighter piece, I used the Shepard monologue. I also found that, when auditioning for a comedy, it was safer to use because it was amusing and not outright funny. Pieces that were supposed to get laughs were always dangerous to use in case they were met with a crushing silence. Egg on face was the last thing I wanted to experience at an audition. The other added bonus to using either piece was that they were not popular, so I could be assured that the people who were listening hadn't already heard these pieces to the point of boredom.

The first production that I auditioned for using one of these was *The Crucible* in Chicago for the part of Abigail. As I recall, I used both to show a contrast of performance, and, yes, to my relief, I actually did get the part!

JOHN CUNNINGHAM

My favorite monologue? The one from *The Seagull* by Anton Chekhov. It is a reply by Trigorin to Nina's fervent statement about him, "You have a beautiful life." This occurs early in act 2. The beauty of this selection for an audition piece is that like all great dramatic writing, it is multilayered. Trigorin is both revealing his rather sour assessment of his life as a famous writer and at the same time seducing Nina. The length is enough to allow the actor a chance to explore the many nooks and crannies of Trigorin's persona.

I've only used it once in an audition for Neil Simon's *The Good Doctor*, on Broadway, but I got the job. More to the point, when I played Trigorin at the Williamstown Theater very early in my career, this speech and the play itself were very revealing of the best means of reaching for art rather than artifice in the theater.

JULIE HARRIS

The monologue I used to audition was just the first part of the girl's dialogue in Tennessee Williams's *This Property Is Condemned*. I think her name is Willie. It's a beautiful piece of writing. She's walking down a railroad track. I used this for auditions when I first came to New York City. I used it when I auditioned for William Liebling and Audrey Wood. Bill Liebling used to send me out on jobs early on in my career.

PHILIP BOSCO

I do have one firm recollection of a monologue and its effect on my life. In high school (St. Peter's Prep, Jersey City, New Jersey — a Jesuit Institution), I came under the influence of a retired professional actor, James Marr, who took me under his wing, so to speak, and used me in the school plays, occasional radio plays, programs, and numerous oratorical and declamation contests connected with the institution. Mr. Marr entered me in a statewide contest held at Princeton University, in which I recited the monologue *Nightmare at Noon* by Stephen Vincent Benet. I remember it as a powerful antiwar piece, which

Mr. Marr felt very strongly about and on which we worked considerably. Chiefly because of his expert coaching and the beauty and effectiveness of the material, I won the contest and felt a great sense of accomplishment and elation. It was an important event in my life.

KEN HOWARD

I recall reciting "Upon the king . . ." from Shakespeare's *Henry V* to land the role of Thomas Jefferson in the musical *1776*. The producer, Stuart Ostrow, had seen me as the Polish cab driver, Karl Kubelik, in *Promises, Promises,* and he needed some assurance that I could handle "highfalutin" language. It worked! When in doubt, always go with the Bard.

DANA IVEY

The first monologue that comes to mind is Katherine's last speech from *The Taming of the Shrew.* I played Katherine (for the first time) in summer stock at the Southern Shakespeare Festival (a short-lived festival) during one of my college summers. We performed in the campus theater of the University of Miami at Coral Gables, I think. During that festival, I also played Hermia in *A Midsummer Night's Dream,* Lady Capulet in *Romeo and Juliet,* and the Duchess of York in *Richard III.* Quite a range for a twenty-year-old! It was a wonderful experience: I learned so much from just the doing of it, and I learned from being around and working with older, more experienced actors. It was my first experience of rotating repertory — a different play each performance — and I still love true rep, though it's hard to find. I learned to crack a bullwhip for the scene with Bianca. I remember standing outside the theater at Rollins College (where I went to school) with a fellow student who was from the Midwest and actually had life experience with bullwhips. He taught me how to crack a whip, though I never attained his proficiency with it. He could stand perfectly still — the motion was all in his wrist. I, however, seemed unable to get much sound from the whip without hurling my whole arm and torso into it. An early lesson in body awareness, isolation, and control.

Years later I played Katherine at the California Shakespeare Festival in Visalia, California (another short-lived festival), and I did the speech for the audience. It's a wonderful speech to learn young and grow with. It makes more sense and takes on layers of meaning, humor, and irony the longer you live with it.

STEPHEN LANG

The monologue with which I secured my first New York employment was *Henry IV, Part I* (act I, scene iii), Hotspur: "My liege, I did deny no prisoners . . ." It was in 1974, for the New York Shakespeare Festival, Anspacher Theater, for Joe Papp and Michael Redman (director) of Sam Waterston's *Hamlet.* Waiting for my turn to audition, I heard the actor before me launch into the speech I was about to do. Against my better judgment, I listened. Redman cut him off partway through. (The actor was Peter Van Norden, who was cast in the show.) When it was my turn and I told them what I planned to do, Redman said to me, "Let's see if you can make it past the 'pouncet box.'" When I got to that section I winked and cut the line, going from "He was perfumed like a milliner" to "And as the soldiers bore dead bodies by . . ." Joe and Michael both laughed, and I was given a role in the show. Years later I did *Death of a Salesman* with Redman, so the monologue paid off, big time. I also used Caliban's "The isle is full of noises" speech sometimes.

JOHN LITHGOW

I'll always love Gallimard's monologue at the end of *Madame Butterfly.* Actually the last ten minutes were very exciting. I feel it was my best moment on stage; my most successful. It involved me changing from a man to a woman, putting on makeup in front of an audience. It's the monologue that John Dexter (the director) asked me to audition with. It's wonderfully written and very exciting to play.

KATE BURTON

My favorite and most successful monologue selections were from *Red Cross* by Sam Shepard (the skiing monologue) and Juliet's "Gallop apace . . ." speech. I used them to get into New York University, Central School of Speech and Drama, American Conservatory Theater, Yale School of Drama, Julliard, and the Williamstown Theater festival. I ended up studying at Yale. I think it was *Red Cross* that made the difference. The Juliet was pretty standard, but the *Red Cross* monologue was exciting and new in the late seventies. I did it on a chair and wore the ski gloves right until the minute when I threw them at Nikos Psacharopoulos and he said, "Oh no, not *Red Cross*!"

LAURENCE LUCKINBILL

I did Mercutio's "Queen Mab" speech (from *Romeo and Juliet*) for Joe Papp, my first season in New York. I got the job of playing Romeo, playing opposite Kathleen Widdoes (who I was already in love with, so that was swell). Of course, Joe fired me a month later. I didn't look like Romeo, he said. But I never wanted to play Romeo anyway, only Mercutio. And Roy Scheider had a lock on that part. So I went back to being a waiter at O'Henry's in the village. But not for long. It was a start, never fired since. Loved Joe in spite of it. P.S., I did Mercutio in college, my first-ever production — they loved me! That's why I chose it; you get to die good.

S. EPATHA MERKERSON

It was for an audition for the John Malkovich production of *Balm in Gilead* by Lanford Wilson. I thought I was auditioning for a replacement, but I was actually auditioning for an understudy role. I was already understudying another show (*Split Second*). I got the understudy role in the Malkovich production but turned it down. The weekend after I turned it down, I saw *Balm in Gilead* and was blown away. The next day I begged them to allow me to do the understudy in *Balm in Gilead*. They gave it to me.

The monologue I used for the audition was from *Ain't Supposed to Die a Natural Death* by Melvin Van Peebles. It's a play about a woman who's going to kill herself. She's going to jump because her life is completely screwed. It had the same feeling as *Balm in Gilead*. It was the first (and only) time I ever did the piece. It was a perfect audition choice. What I like about the piece is that her desperation freed me. Her words belie what she's saying. I also like the repetition in the writing. Yvette Hawkins suggested the monologue for that audition. I've always appreciated that suggestion.

JOE MONTELLO

A favorite monologue of mine is from *Angels in America*. When I first read it, I was overwhelmed. There was an incredible amount of information. It felt like I was reading another language. It's convoluted and complex. Tony Kushner (the playwright) said I should approach it as simply a technical exercise in rhythm and pace.

One thing I learned in rehearsal and then later in performance was how funny it was. I had no idea. The secret to doing the piece is to just try to make the points. You must stay ahead of the audience. Think of it as like learning a dance. Take it slow at first, and after you've memorized the steps, just go with it. It may feel terrifying at first, but it's very musical, and you'll see it'll just take you. When I finally got it and was performing it, it was exhilarating! And once I trusted that I knew what I was doing, it became effortless.

DYLAN BAKER

When pursuing work while in college, I was attracted to summer Shakespeare festivals. The work took me to Colorado, Maine, and Virginia and brought me in touch with actors, directors, and designers that have come in and out of my life time and again. Auditions required verse monologues, and I always had a few available. Prince Hal, Romeo, and Benedict were standbys, but I started to have good results with Edgar's speech in *King Lear,* act II, scene iii. Auditions can be so sterile — a cold room, suits, small talk. I always loved Edgar's frenzy to change the mood and energy in the room. As he thinks to take on the shape of a beast, I would unbutton my shirt sleeves and root about on the floor in the pursuit of twigs and nails. Edgar's trying to change himself, hide his identity from his own family, and I was trying to prove to the suits that I could do that, too! After disheveled poor Tom, I'd follow it up with some comic piece where the guy's uptight about his appearance, which would give me a chance to tuck my shirt in, unknot my "elf'd hairs," and pull myself together for the inevitable follow-up chit-chat.

ALISON FRASER

My first audition in New York City was for the female understudy in a musical version of Tom Eyen's hit, *The Dirtiest Show in Town.* I *was* green as green can be, but Tom and his composer Henry Krieger couldn't have been more supportive as they put me through my paces. About halfway through the lengthy audition process, Tom handed me a typewritten speech to read cold. And a few hours later I learned I had landed not the understudy role, but a new part he'd written just for me. I will always credit him with giving me the initial boost of self-confidence one so desperately needs to take the plunge into the New York theater scene. He was a fabulous guy, a singular talent, and is missed sorely.

BRIAN MURRAY

My favorite audition monologue is from Shakespeare's *King Henry VI, Part III*. It's the role of the Son (in some versions he's called "The Boy Who Killed His Father"). The speech I'm referring to is in act II, scene iv. It's simple and has a great deal of emotion. I was doing television in England, and Peter Wood suggested that I do it for an audition for Stratford-on-Avon. What's wonderful about the piece is it's short — about fourteen lines — with very simple verse. It's early Shakespeare. It's a perfect audition piece for those actors who are afraid to do Shakespeare. Also a woman can do this piece as well as a man.

FRANCES STERNHAGEN

My first audition piece was Sonya's speech from *Uncle Vanya* by Anton Chekhov. It's the speech right after she's just spent time with Astrov, and she's thrilled that he talked to her. Then she vacillates between misery that she's so plain to excitement that he spent time with her to the realization that he probably doesn't love her. I was trying to get into a professional acting company, and I used this speech along with four other audition pieces. This was in Boston, and I was teaching at the time. The man holding the audition said to me, "Miss Hagen, if you want to be an actress, you should give up teaching because you do everything as if you're leading the Girl Scouts onto the hockey field." Well that made me mad! Mad enough to do just that! I gave up teaching and started trying to get work as an actress. I finally did get into Arena Stage.

My most successful audition was when I auditioned for *Equus*. I memorized the mother's speech in the second act with the psychiatrist. She says that Alan is himself. Whatever she did, she did the best she could, and even though you don't believe in a devil, she does. In essence, she's saying, "The devil made him do it." I wanted that play so much. I knew I was right for the part, and so I memorized it, even though I held the script in my hand. Maybe that's why I got it.

KIM HUNTER

I have hardly ever auditioned with a monologue. My very first audition was for a play being cast, so I read with the stage manager from the play itself. All my auditions have followed the same pattern — even to the present day. I did perform a monologue of sorts my senior year in high school. It was a composite of Dorothy Parker writings, lasting about half an hour. I put it together myself but, sadly, never preserved a copy.

ELAINE STRITCH

I was only nineteen years old when I performed Mrs. Chisholm from *The Petrified Forest* by Robert Sherwood. She is supposed to be forty-five years old or so. It was a summer stock production directed by my drama teacher Irwin Picator. The monologue I'm thinking of begins: "You haven't the vaguest notion of what goes on inside me." It's straightforward and to the point and has pathos and humor and laughs. By the way, Marlon Brando played Bo and Walter Matthau was Duke Mantee. What a beginning, eh?!

ELI WALLACH

My favorite monologues are from *The Harmfulness of Tobacco* (the Lecturer, who begins "Ladies, and so to speak, gentlemen") by Chekhov and a piece from *Swan* Song (Svetlovidov, who begins "Well, what do you know about that?") also by Chekhov. These two pieces really give an actor a workout. I highly recommend them!

AMY WRIGHT

My favorite monologue was the one I did in *Fifth of July* ("I'm the greatest"). I really love that speech. I did from the first time I read it. And as it turned out, it was a real showstopper; the audience always laughed. It's one of those monologues that starts off slow and has a great build. It's very, very funny.

HELEN HANFT

I have two favorite monologues. They both concern women who made the wrong choices. The first one is a monologue I call "Friends" from *Why Hanna's Skirt Won't Stay Down* by Tom Eyen. I played a woman who used her sexuality as a substitute for love, and therefore only found men who used, abused, and abandoned her. She joins a social club and meets an atypical man. He is short and not handsome, but he satisfies Hanna; he maintains her. Unfortunately, Hanna becomes bored with such a decent guy. She goes to the club looking for him one night, and when asked, "Do you mean the funny guy with the wobbly walk? The older not-so-handsome guy?" she replies, "No! No! I mean the one who loved me!" Through her own self-destructiveness, she loses the only thing she ever really loved.

The second monologue is *Helen* from the original monologue book, *Streettalk: Original Character Monologues* by Glenn Alterman. Helen is a housewife from Queens who marries out of a desperate need for security. She's been married for twenty years and is bored to tears. One night, while her husband is sleeping, she hears a knock at the door. It's Hal, her handsome, charming, new next-door neighbor who is two inches tall. She invites him in, he sits on her coffee cup saucer, and they talk into the night, realizing they are soulmates. Eventually they decide to run off together. God bless both the late Mr. Eyen and the very present Mr. Alterman for these two gems.

DEBRA MONK

One of my favorite monologues is from Lanford Wilson's *Redwood Curtain*. Actually, Lanford wrote the piece for me. I call it "the car monologue." It's at the top of the play. It's so beautifully written. I always enjoyed doing it. *Redwood Curtain* was a very special play for me: I won the Tony for it.

MILO O'SHEA

The selection that I most love is *The Selfish Giant* by Oscar Wilde. I always find it deeply moving — even as a child when I first heard it. I could never pass by the Wilde home on Merrion Square, Dublin, on my way to school, without thinking of it.

SADA THOMPSON

I haven't done a monologue in years. But there is one from *U.S.A.* that'll always be special to me. It's the long Isadora Duncan monologue late in the play. I always enjoyed doing it. Also I did a monologue from *Riders to the Sea* by John Synge to get into Carnegie Tech.

DAVID MARGULIES

My first audition piece was a Shakespeare, oddly, though it got me a job as an understudy for the New York Shakespeare Festival. I've forgotten whether it was Hamlet or Hotspur. My most memorable audition was for Bob Fosse for *All That Jazz*. I came into one of those dance studios that Fosse loved. There were big windows facing the side street, a radiator running under them. Fosse was alone in the room with Robert Alane Aurther, who had written the script with him and was the coproducer. We spoke, and then I began the wedding ceremony from Jules Feiffer's *Little Murders*. I played to Fosse and Aurther and to the imaginary wedding guests in the bare studio room. Fosse was perched atop the radiator, his laserlike attention and keen pleasure boosted by my pleasure. It was fun. I got the job.

TOVAH FELDSHUH

The monologue I used that won me the McKnight Fellowship in Acting to the Tyrone Guthrie Theater was from Bertolt Brecht's *Good Woman of Setzuan*. It was Shen Te's monologue when she realizes she is pregnant. It begins with the line, "Oh joy, a new human being is on the way" and ends with her singing, "For he gobbled up the plum." I chose this piece because I was able to show my acting skills combined with mime and singing. It is not a commonly used piece and, if done well, can stop the conveyor belt of competition.

MICHAEL YORK

I remember very well my first audition speech to yield significant results. In fact, the occasion was so momentous that I described it in my recent autobiography *Accidentally on Purpose*. The actual speech was Hamlet's "O that this too, too solid flesh" one. Of course, the best advice to any actor is also Hamlet's — and I'm not referring to his excellent and practical advice to the players. It comes later and applies to life in general: "If it be now, 'tis not to come; if it be not to come, it will be now; if it be not now, yet it will come, the readiness is all."

For my first professional engagement at the Dundee Repertory Theatre in Scotland in 1964, I again auditioned with Shakespeare — Romeo's final speech and John of Lancaster's peroration in Gaultree Forest in *Henry IV, Part 2* (act IV, scene i). The latter, "You are well encounter'd here, my cousin Mowbray," has the advantage of being relatively unfamiliar and yet showy and authoritative.

To become a member of Britain's National Theatre Company, I auditioned for that august, uncommon man Laurence Olivier, with the irreverent Common Man from Robert Bolt's *A Man for All Seasons*.

chapter 12

Audition Monologues

What follows are an assortment of audition monologues that you might want to try working on for your next audition. Much appreciation to the playwrights who offered their wonderful words for this chapter.

NASTY LITTLE SECRETS by Lanie Robertson

Kenneth Halliwell, Joe Orton's lover, describes his mother's death.

KENNETH
any age
seriocomic

Oh, we never went near the water. Because she was such a large woman, I guess. I doubt if father ever saw her totally naked. Or she him. We'd cart baskets of food, though, with . . . everything. The last time, she'd fixed this plateful of orange wedges, and there were all these wasps flying about, drawn by the citrus, I suppose. I'd wave them away and then run off. It was a game we were playing. Father'd gone off on one of his walks somewhere. We were laughing and it was very fair, very . . . beautiful. I was running back to her and she said something I couldn't hear. As I got closer she lifted a piece of orange and popped it in her mouth. When she'd lifted it I'd seen two wasps settle on it, and it seemed so funny to me, her eating the wasps, I immediately thought of all kinds of things to tease her with, such as roasted wasp, and wasps in cream sauces. That sort of thing. She started clawing her throat and her eyes teared up, and she fell back off of the chair onto the sand. Her swollen tongue forced her mouth open. I remember hearing the wind and sounds of people calling one another in the distance. Her face had turned orange and her eyes were still open. I remember listening to the wind. Then I sat down in the sand. Staring.

• • •

A KISS TO BUILD A DREAM ON by Joe Pintauro

Boomer and Marianna Curry, professors at a liberal arts college, are faithfully in love through twenty-five years of marriage. When Marianna is diagnosed with a fatal disease, Boomer tries to trick himself out of grief by jumping into an affair with Charlotte, a college employee. Marianna, discovering the shame, not merely of her illness, but of her husband's cowardice, consults the chaplain, a Jesuit, who eventually falls in love with her. When Marianna asks to leave with the priest, who promises to care for her, Boomer is forced by jealousy to claw his way back to the real love he is hiding from and the loss of it.

First Monologue

BOOMER
fifty
dramatic

She tried to step away toward the water, surrendering, falling . . . She didn't seem to feel the cold. Didn't matter. And she actually . . . tried to swim, so pathetically, her feet splashing as if to kick away all that had been her life, including me. When the splashing stopped, the water became smooth and there was no sight of her except . . . there . . . her hair like seaweed on the surface. I waited long enough for her to have her way, then I walked out to her, shoes, trousers. It wasn't deep. I lifted her and saw the moon twice in her eyes, two moons, so eerie and beautiful, no breath, just a smile of certainty on her face. Her vultures flew off. Sorry. I was proud of her carelessness, her nerve, her inner strength. No doctors, no mourners, just a couple of crows in a tree and she as pure as a saint all wet in the moonlight. The water supported her in my arms and I put my cheek against hers. "Here we are again on the water, weightless and drifting, like a couple of kids again." She felt so thin and young in my arms. What are we doing in the lake in October in Vermont? Two adolescents doing the craziest thing in the moonlight. I knew that outside her memory, I have little existence. I could almost feel her memory rising up to the moon like a puff of smoke, like a puff of smoke . . . and me with it.

Second Monologue

Charlotte is Boomer's mistress.

CHARLOTTE
forty
dramatic

I know he's using me. You think I don't know he's using me?
But would you use me? No. What reason would you have to
use me? But him, his wife is dying. The twenty-five-year love
of his whole life is about to go off the cliffs into oblivion and
you don't stop loving people who are gonna die. You love them
more. But sex scares him with her, love scares him with her.
That's why he runs to me. He's running from the biggest love
of his life and the biggest grief of his life. He hides inside me.
So I became Miss Sloppy Seconds on a five-percent hope that
he sees something in me, I never saw in myself, couldn't see in
myself even if it was there. Maybe it's nothing, just me being
there, being there, being there. You know, he's not ashamed to
cry in front of me. Is he gonna cry in front of her? I'm the one
puts up with his narcissism, his whining, and for that alone he'll
probably turn around and marry me, out of . . . I don't know,
fear of living? You know, he's gorgeous. On the outside, in
spades, but his broken heart made him gorgeous in his chest,
in here and I'm the one puts who my head on that chest so don't
tell me he's using me. So don't even think I don't love him. It's
glued to my insides, it burns in here and let it burn a hole right
through me. There's nothing anywhere near like him ever gonna
cross my path. If he takes off what happens to an anybody like
me? I stay what I am. An anybody who has nobody. And don't
tell me I don't sound like myself anymore. I don't wanna sound
like myself. Don't wanna be myself. I'm desecrating my inno-
cence. You're absolutely right. It's so obscene and degrading it's
killing me and I say, let it. You said I should love myself, like
that's enough? You can get by on loving yourself? You tell me

I should come first. That is bullshit. That doesn't work. You lose that way. You lose everything. Don't you know that? So it's no news that he's using me. You know what I say? Thank God he's using me. OK? Thank God.

• • •

FORGETTING FRANKIE by Annie Evans

Felice has recently learned her fiancé Gary was also engaged to two other women. She dumped him and spent the next month doing baking therapy. She is talking on the telephone.

FELICE
late twenties
comic

I was voting. I always vote. I go in, I go up to the lady. She finds my card, I sign my name. It's primaries so no one's there, I go right in, pull the little thingy, the curtain closes, I look up at the names — I never heard of anyone. Well, I do. I pay attention to this stuff. I read the little sheets they have on who's running. But, you see? How this breakup has made me? I totally forgot you have to know who to vote for. You have to make a decision. I felt myself starting to cry, and I said no. No way. No more crying, no more baking, no more horror videos, no more dark glasses. I can't believe I did this, but I did. I pushed open the curtain and screamed — who are these people! Yes, my hands were shaking, but I couldn't stop. I said I don't know who these people are! Can you tell me who they are?! At first, it was to everyone, then it was to the next person in line. He was standing right there and I had to talk to someone. No, the thing is, would you wait, the thing is, he was laughing at me. Laughing. He showed me, yes, he had one of those sheets and we went through it together. Then, we went next door and got a cup of coffee. A-huh, and we discussed the public education system, and the death of the Board of Estimates. God, I'd forgotten, you know? What do you mean, did I get his number? He was married. Yes, married, you're missing the whole point. Oh shoot, hold on. *(Felice presses the receiver.)* Hello? Oh — God — Yeh — No, no I won't. Yes — Hold on, all right — *(She presses the receiver.)* It's Gary. Can you believe it? Yes, he's holding. No, I won't do that. *(Laughs.)* Not that either. It's OK.

● ● ●

ANNIE-MAY by Glenn Alterman

Annie-May recalls a terrifying date.

ANNIE-MAY
late teens
seriocomic

I showed up at the diner over a half hour early. I was so nervous. Well you know, you saw, I was a wreck. Got a booth in the back. Margo came over, asked me what I wanted. Ordered some coffee. Caffeine, just what I needed, right? I started bouncin' back an' forth in the booth. Margo asked if I was all right. I said "Sure, have a date, little nervous." "Date?" she said. "Well, la-de-da." She's was bein' so smug, wanted to smack her. Hate her sometimes, don't you? Didn't dare tell her it was someone I met on the Internet. She told me I looked nice. Asked if my dress was new. "Just bought it, Laytons." "Stylish," she said. "Pretty." "Margo," I said, "don't you have any other customers?" "Sorry," she said. "Have a nice date."

She left, and there I was alone with my nerves. Kept lookin' out the window, waitin'. Seemed like hours, I'm tellin' ya. Then I heard a car pull into the parking lot. Car door opened, than shut. I couldn't breathe, Linda, I tell ya, I could not breathe! Door to the diner opened. It was him, I just knew it! I didn't dare turn around. Wanted it to be like a movie moment; ya know, Julia Roberts meets Richard Gere. Then he touched me, Linda, my right shoulder. I slowly turned, my smile, prepared and ready. My well-rehearsed, "Why Bob, how nice to finally meet you." But when I looked up, there was this much older man! He said, "You Annie-May?" I said, "Yes," but I wanted to say, "Who are you? Where's Bob? You his father?"

He sat down next to me. I couldn't move, couldn't talk. He was as old as my father! Stringy white hair, fat, ugly, with thick, dark glasses. He lied, Linda! That picture he sent musta been takin' a hundred years ago. He had yellow-stained teeth, looked like fangs. And his dirty fingers looked like claws. He was old, I was scared! "Wanna go for a ride?" he said. His breath stunk, halitosis. "Ride? Car? You?"

Margo came over, smiled, said, "They finally fixed the toilet. Remember, you asked me to tell you when they fixed it?" I caught her cue, turned to Bob, said "Be right back." Went with Margo to the kitchen. She started laughin', said "Is Grandpa your date?" She opened the back door, let me out. I ran home fast as I could. My new dress was a mess. Collapsed on my bed, cried hysterical. Then I went to my computer, sent Bob a "So long, you're a big liar!" e-mail.

He was the date from hell. I'm tellin' ya Linda, my dream date was a real nightmare.

• • •

SACRED JOURNEY by Mathew Witten

Sacred Journey *is based on interviews with a Native American man who lives on the streets of a big city in the United States. He has bright eyes and a warm smile.*

JOHN
thirty-five
dramatic

(Grins.) But maybe my Creator heard my prayers. Because last year I'm on the street, my clothes all dirty, needing a shower, drunk . . . And I look up and there's this woman walking along. Dressed up real nice, looking sharp. "Oh, shit." I put my head down. *(Puts his head down; pulls a cap over his eyes.)* But this woman walks right up to me. "Is that you, John?"

"Hi, Marie." I hadn't seen her for ten years. Hell, I thought she was still in Michigan!

So she goes into the store to buy something, and I tell this Korean guy, "Gimme some roses." "Gimme some money." And I grab some red roses. And when Marie comes out of the store, *(Offers roses.)* "Pretty roses for a pretty lady." She just shakes her head. "John, you haven't changed." But she smiles, you know? And she takes the roses.

I ask her, "What are you doing here?!" She won't say, but she tells me about our sons. My older son, he knows, like five languages and science and math. He's in a special program for gifted children. And my younger son, he's dancing in the Nutcracker Ballet. That's, like the most famous ballet in the world. Ands he dances at powwows. "Marie, I'd like to see my sons." Well, I don't know what they would like, and . . . I don't know." So she goes away.

Then a week later it just happens that I'm sober, and I took a shower and this guy I know on the street gives me some nice-looking clothes and a job selling hardware. So I'm standing behind the counter and Marie comes in with this kid. Only he's like a young man, six feet tall, taller than me. I say, "Hi, Marie." And this young man says "Hi, Dad." *(Beat.)* You're my son?"

I say to my boss, "This is my son. I haven't seen him in ten years." My boss says, "Take a lunch break." And he gives me twenty-five bucks. So I take my son to a Chinese restaurant, and he tells me all about those languages he's studied, and biology and physics. And he knows a lot about the Indian people. And he's proud. He's a proud young Indian man. And I just . . . this is my son.

And I'm so glad I'm wearing nice clothes and I don't smell bad, and I'm not drunk, and I have the money for the Chinese restaurant. I say, "Marie, may I see my other son?" "I don't know if he'd like to just yet." "OK. Tell him I love him and I understand." And I say to my son, "I wish I had more wisdom to teach you. But I'm glad you're proud to be an Indian man. Always be proud." And he says, "Thanks, Dad." And he hugs me. And then he and his mother walk down the street. *(Overcome by emotion.)* I'm so proud. *(Smiles proudly for a couple of beats, then checks himself and says dryly, in a flat voice.)* So I celebrate. With some Thunderchicken. Thunderchicken and vodka.

• • •

MERMAID'S BLOOD by Ty Adams

Ferrell Buck talks to a young intern working at a small museum and explains where the drops of water on the floor are coming from.

FERRELL
sixties
dramatic

You ask, What makes this painting I've done so many times, a dead mermaid on the beach, what makes This One . . . different? Well, I can tell you to look on the floor below the painting. You'll see drops of water. A thousand times I've awakened, looked in the mirror, decided not to shave, downed a cup of coffee . . . and sat down to paint. And a thousand and one begins as the first, nothing different; I stare at the empty canvas until my forehead is bleeding. Then I begin; all the initial strokes are familiar, but I go on . . . suddenly my tongue begins to move my teeth and I discover I'm imitating each muscle, each fish scale along the mermaid's legs and fin; my eyebrows get into the act; I'm painting her neck now; my tongue moves to imitate; I'm painting her hip now with its special curve; I follow that curve and as I paint, I suddenly feel a tense curve in my own hip; my concentration gets keener now as I move to her hair and down to her breasts . . . there's a bit of seaweed across the nipple; I can feel the pain; my nipple feels the pain; I paint the seaweed slightly lifted to the side of the nipple to relieve the pain; as I paint . . . the pain goes away. I'm painting her nostrils now; the nostrils are nudged into the beach sand; the sand is dry and I feel my nose twitch; her nostril seems to loose its last breath, an exhale tosses dust into the air; I WANT TO PAINT DUST; I feel a sneeze coming on from the dust. It's distracting. I stop painting, wait for the sneeze; I'm anxious to get back to my painting so I twitch my nose to encourage the sneeze. It works. My eyelids begin blinking rapidly and my head raises itself; my neck tightens; briefly I struggle against the sneeze but it's too late; I turn away from the painting and the energy from my depths comes bellowing out and an accidental brush stroke strikes the canvas . . . creating a wound.

• • •

NIGHT VISITS by Simon Fill

Tom is a witty young medical resident during his thirty-fifth hour on call. He and a patient are in an examining room. Because he's just helped her cope with her father's death, she asks him who he knows who died.

TOM
late twenties
seriocomic

(*Beat.*) My wife Katherine. She was a nurse here in pediatrics. We grew up together in Brooklyn, but in high school I was too shy to ask her out. We ran into each other when she'd graduated from college, at a reading of James Joyce by an Irish actor. Joyce was her favorite writer. She and I dated. At that point, I was well on my way to becoming the "funny doctor." She was quiet and funnier, in that good way the most serious people are. After two months, I proposed. Now that was funny. She didn't answer. We kept dating. Every day for two months after that I proposed. Silence. I thought, "This woman either likes me or is totally insensate." At the end of that time she gave me a copy of *Finnegans Wake*, her favorite book. At college I'd read it and almost finished. The first page, that is. But I loved her so much I slogged though the book. Boy, did I love her. On page fifty, at the bottom, in pencil, someone'd written something. I looked closely. It said, "Yes. I'll marry you." *(Pause.)* I called her up and told her Joyce had accepted my proposal of marriage. *(Pause.)* She was driving to Riverdale, a favor, to pick up a friend's kid at school. I know she was starting to think about children herself. She said she wanted them to have "my looks and her sense of humor." Another car, an old lady who shouldn't have been driving, who had a history of epilepsy . . . and . . . you know the rest. The other woman lived. *(Beat.)* I asked Katie once why she wrote "yes" to me on page fifty. She said, "I knew you loved me, but I wasn't sure how much." *(Pause.)* Don't look so serious.

• • •

SOLACE by Glenn Alterman

Sam joyfully recalls the day that his son was born.

SAM
fifties or sixties
seriocomic

(Smiling.) We were waiting in the waiting room, Sadie and me. Had been there for hours, driving each other nuts. Finally, the nurse comes out, big smile, calls me over, and says, "You his father?" "His? Father?! YES!!" "Healthy baby boy!" she says, "Healthy baby boy."

It's a boy, BOOM, it's a boy! "I've got a son," I say to Sadie. "I got a son!" Sadie and me, hug and kiss. "Mazel tov, mazel tov!"

Then the nurse brings him out. And let me tell ya, let-me-tell-you, the first time you see your son, NOTHIN' matches that! A miracle! *(Joyfully.)* This fat, little, butterball. Little fingers, little toes. Ya get emotional! Sadie starts to cry, nurse starts to laugh. "S'my son!" I say to Sadie. "S'my son! "S'my grandson," she boasts. "My grandson!" I'm handing out cigars, pissin' in my pants. Sadie starts to laugh, I start to cry. Mazel tov! Mazel tov! Little fingers, little hands.

You feel so . . . ! You feel . . . ! *(Softly, smiling.)* What a god-damned day that was, what a god-damned day!

• • •

RUNNING QUARTER HORSES by Mary Sue Price

First Monologue

June. Hot. Just outside Miami, Oklahoma. Bobby, a professional bull rider, is just out of the hospital where he spent the past six months recovering from massive injuries, including a broken back, sustained at the National Finals Rodeo where he was bucked off and stomped by a bull. It was his seventh and final trip to the National Finals, where he had been the favorite to win. Rodeo cost him his wife, his daughter, all his money, his health, and almost his life. Bobby has returned to give his ex-wife, a retired champion barrel racer, all he has left: a first-rate quarter horse, won on a bet. If she takes the horse, he can't help believing she'll take him back, too.

BOBBY
forties
dramatic

BOBBY: Right before the buzzer, in that last second of a real good ride, everything gets clear. Your free hand's back and the bull's bucking good and you don't even have to think, you know? You sink right down into him, like you are him. Everything gets real quiet. You don't look down, no matter what. You float. *(Beat.)* When I woke up and realized that I wasn't really living out here . . .
[DANA: I shouldn't have ever told you that stuff.]
The last time, except for rodeo, I took a real good ride was with you.
[DANA: You're good. I'll bet your little darlins' suck that right up.]
That isn't what I mean.
[DANA: Thanks.]
It doesn't have anything to do with —
[DANA: I remember some pretty lean nights myself. *(Beat.)*]
One time we were driving some place out in West Texas, I think, or maybe Kansas on the way to Denver because the road is real straight and nobody's on it but us. It's before Emmy was born and your horse is shuffling around in the trailer and I know we're going to have to stop before too long and let him stretch his legs. But I don't want to wake you up. You're sleeping right up next to me and it's so dark I have to double-check to be sure the brights are on. But there's this little crack of light on the horizon. The sun is getting ready to come up and I'm rolling right into it, fast as I can go. Then you wake up a little bit and tell me to slow down and I say OK and let up some and you go back to sleep and it all falls together and I'm the only person in the world and I'm way out on my own, but I'm connected to the only other person I will ever really need and because of that, I'm connected to everything. *(Beat.)* We could have that again. Me and you in the front seat. Emmy up in the bunk.

Dragging this horse. Living a life together. We could win so big.
(Bobbie kisses her.) Marry me.
[DANA: Marry you?]
You married me once.
[DANA: What's the matter with you?]
We could make it work.

Second Monologue

*Dana Billings is a retired barrel racer, successful horse trainer,
and two-time National Finals winner. She divorced Bobby several years ago and is raising Emmy, their twelve-year-old daughter, on a farm she bought with her own money. It's the place
she and Bobby always dreamed of living. She's engaged to marry
an old high school friend. Bobby has shown up out of nowhere.
She's still in love with him but knows he'll mess up her life if
she lets him back in. Bobby thinks she hasn't seen him since
before the accident. Chance is Emmy's horse, not the horse
Bobby wants to give Dana.*

DANA
forties
dramatic

I went to see you in the hospital.
[BOBBY: When?]
Christmas week. Right after they moved you from Vegas to
Houston. Emmy wanted to come with me but she hadn't seen
you since Amarillo.
[BOBBY: I took her out to that steak place.]
You'd won real big. All the guys went with you. You let her
order that seventy-two ounce steak she's seen advertised on the
highway all her life.
[BOBBY: It's what she wanted.]
Emmy felt like the sweetheart of the rodeo that night. *(Beat.)*

Some doctor told me you wouldn't live through New Year. I didn't want Emmy to see you hurt that bad. Anyway. I flew to Houston. *(Beat.)* I wasn't about to walk through a waiting room full of your girlfriends and hungover cowboys. I went late at night. Way past visiting hours. I told the head nurse I was your ex. She just looked at me. Nobody cared. *(Beat.)* You were by yourself. All these tubes. Machines. You looked already dead. *(Beat.)* I gave you an ice chip and put some Vaseline on your lips. They were almost bleeding. I kissed your eyelids. You groaned. I didn't touch you again. *(Beat.)* I stayed a long time. I read you the Twenty-third Psalm and this story from the *Daily Oklahoman* about what a courageous athlete you had been. They acted like you were already dead. I couldn't think of what else to say. So I told you all about this place. How the creek runs wide at the bottom of the hill. And the second story windows leak sometimes. And how the light falls on the porch early in the morning. I told you how to get here from the turnpike. And how you walk straight into the kitchen from the front porch and the whole place smells like wood smoke all winter long. I told you I'm putting in fescue for hay. And that when Emmy goes flying across the back field on Chance, she reminds me of you. *(Beat.)* I left around daybreak. *(Beat.)* It was so hot in Houston. It didn't seem like Christmas. I hadn't slept for a couple of days. I'd rented a car. I couldn't find it in the parking garage. I couldn't even remember what color it was. This security guard tried to help. We finally called Avis for a description. I flew home. I got my crying done on the plane. Most of it. I told Emmy you probably wouldn't live. We prayed for you. *(Beat.)* I called the hospital every couple of days. They took you off the critical list. I thought you'd call. So did Emmy. We tried a lot of times but we couldn't get through. She'd always end up crying. I didn't push it. I called you a time or two, late at night. The line was always busy or nobody picked up. I could have called Tuff, tracked you down, but what for? You didn't want to talk to either one of us. Emmy stopped asking about you. She's been working real hard with Chance. That helps. She used to take the cell phone out to the barn with her. But now she doesn't.

Third Monologue

Later in the play, Bobby and Dana have not been able to connect. The horse is on its way, but Bobby's about to leave and tell the driver to take the horse back to New Mexico. Bobby doesn't know when, or if, he'll be back. Dana has turned down his spontaneous marriage proposal.

DANA
forties
dramatic

So you're walking away again.
[BOBBY: What do you want me to do?]
I want you to be proud of me. To be glad I bought this place and got on with my own life. I want you to realize that I'm raising a real nice kid with no help from you. To see that you aren't some hero because you send your child support. I want you to understand why I can't just take this horse with no warning and no time to think about it. I want it to be like our dream and for nothing terrible to have happened. I want to live out here with you, don't you get that? I want it to be before you got hurt. I want you to call me and Emmy and invite us to the National Finals to see your last ride. Don't you know I wanted to be there? But you were on a roll. I was afraid I'd break it. I wanted you to win so bad. I wanted you to know that feeling that, for that one night, nobody in the world is better. I want you not to have to try so hard and never get what you need the most. *(Beat.)* I want you to love me like I am now and I don't know if you can do that or not. Five years ago if you'd given me this horse? We'd be rolling around in the barn by now. I would have believed every word you said and been glad to see you even if

I knew you were going to leave. But that isn't enough, Bobby. Not anymore. And this is my place, not ours. I don't know if I want to deal with that. Or this horse. Or you. And I want you to kiss me again. Dammit.

• • •

UNCLE PHILIP'S COAT by Matty Selman

In many respects, Uncle Philip's Coat *is a memory play. One actor portrays the many faces in his family. The main relationship in this piece is that of two brothers:Mickey, a successful jeweler, and his* luftmensch, *wandering brother, Philip. In this monologue, Mickey talks to his son about Philip, who survived a Russian pogrom but was left traumatized by the memory.*

MICKEY
fifties or older
dramatic

See this . . . do you know what this is . . . ? This is where a Cossack's bayonet missed your uncle's heart by two inches . . . *(A pause, then —)* You ever wonder why your uncle wore this coat . . . why he never let go of it . . . why he lived the way he lived and never led a normal life . . . ? Philip and I were *visionateh* . . . the ones who saved themselves.. We survived the Mykolayiv Pogrom . . . Philip was nine and I was four . . . we had never been separated once our whole life . . . we slept together in a little loft bed that my father made . . . I couldn't sleep if Philip wasn't there . . . I felt safe having him near me . . . So, we went to bed that night . . . it was, I think, mid-October. It was very cold . . . drafty . . . Baba was stuffing towels — dishtowels she used to stuff into the walls and under the door and around the windows . . . to keep the cold out . . . . . and the next thing I remember is being jolted awake by this noise . . . this loud squealing and whining . . . I'd never heard anything like it . . . they were butchering the animals . . . cows, and geese . . . and dogs . . . they were butchering dogs . . . and I look up and there's Baba's face and she's not saying a word . . . she just scoops me up and pulls Philip down the little stepladder from the bed . . . and we're running . . . running with her along the hall . . . the house is pitch-black and I hear men yelling outside with explosions and horse's hooves . . . Baba pulls open the door to the front closet and pushes Philip inside . . . he's hanging onto her skirt: "*Baba! ich hob moy're . . . ich hob moy're . . .*" she unhooks his fingers from her skirt: '*Shtill, mine kind . . . shtill!* . . . then she takes this coat down . . . pulls out the hanger . . . and sticks it into the sleeves of Philip's nightshirt right over his arms . . . wraps the coat around him and pulls it up over his head and buttons it all the way up, covering him . . . she takes a chunk of black bread from her apron pocket and puts it in his mouth, he shouldn't scream . . . then . . . with all her might, she picks Philip up in the coat and hangs him in the closet and . . . for a second I'm watching him swing there back and forth . . . and then . . . bam! She shuts the door on him and runs with me to the kitchen . . . we had a false wall behind the stove . . . she pulls back two wooden panels and takes me in her arms, I couldn't breathe . . . she's holding me against her breasts so tight . . . I could hear her heart beating so fast *biddibum-biddibum* . . . and she closes us in this tiny, dark space . . . and then . . . we hear them coming up the path . . . breaking down the door . . . stomping . . . smashing . . . "*Eedee Bahat' Zhid! Bahat Zhid! Zhid! Zhid! Zhid!*" They're smashing everything in the house and breaking down all the doors . . . we can hear the sound of fabric being stabbed by knives . . . tearing . . . . shredding sounds . . . they're in the closet . . . they're killing Philip!

• • •

EASTVILLE by Ellen Lewis

Eastville *takes place in 1859, on Harriet Tubman's Underground Railroad. It's the evening Harriet Tubman goes through Sag Harbor on her way to Connecticut instead of her traditional route upstate New York. Tubman ends up at the house of a black whaler, Cuffee, and his wife, Christine. The whaler and his wife are runaway slaves. In this monologue, Harriet Tubman is remembering her escape from slavery.*

HARRIET
any age
dramatic

I hire myself out like you, Christine. I go to the market. I make a good bargain. I buy me two steers for the price of one. I bring them steer home, and march them all sassy like, all over the yard — talking about "look what I got for my man, my man, Tubman, he's a free man," all up in this Mandinka woman — face. Oh she don't take too well to that, now do she? Gets all jealous like them Mandinka get.

Mandinka woman, she makes up some story about, how I must have stole, to get me two steer, cause she ain't never hear, two for the price of one. She whisper to Master, like she going to be his forever friend — she say, "that them Ashanti . . ." that's me, I'm Ashanti . . . "Are nothing but thieves and liars — always have been."

McCracken send Boss, he's the overseer, down to the quarters with his disputin' chair — that ole eagle, I call him an eagle, cause when he gets in a fury he takes these claws made of iron, and he uses them to hold us to the nearest tree, for days sometimes — mostly hours though.

So you know what that ole eagle do? He takes one of his mean spirited bulls from out back and put, it, me and that Mandinka woman, fence us in to fight it out. He tells everyone to gather so's he can teach a lesson —

He says, "I'm going to let God sort this one, we'll see who's the liar here and that will be that." He put me in the fence, he put the Mandinka woman in the fence, and he put the bull in the fence, and lock the door — for a moment we all forgot our uproar and stare at that ole bull. No bull was going to stop an Ashanti woman from a Mandinka woman, and I get to fightin' — only every time I have at that fight that bull bend over, point his horns and charges — I got to take the hand that holds her throat, and use it to push back the bull — that bull ain't going to have at my fight.

I'm hittin' and jumpin', holding back the bull — hittin' and dodgin' and hittin' again — everybody scatter out from the charge — scatter in for the fight, out from the charge, in for the fight . . . in out, in out, in out . . . Ashanti — Mandinka — Ashanti — Mandinka, and that ole eagle watching and holding tight on to them iron claws. This go on and on 'til me and the Mandinka woman can't get to settling cause the bull keep getting' in my way. Me, and that Mandinka woman, look each other straight in the eye and nod — agreeing.

We get on either side of that bull — side up to him like this, and don't you know, before anyone can look, we got one hand on his horn, like this, and the other under his neck.

Everybody shouting, and cheering us as we take that mean feisty bull down on one leg, and shout the cries of war *(shout)*, we take that ole bull down on the other leg, and shout praises to the ancestors *(shout)*, we snatch them back two legs, and shout to the Ashanti *(shout)*, the bull goes down, and with the thunder of each stroke, as we sing the chant of the Yoruba, and we shout to the Mandinka, and we shout to the Ashanti, the Masi — we shout to the great coming together to bring down that bull.

I feel the praises and shouts rumble through my body. I'm moved to a dance I ain't never felt the likes of before. I was raised straight up in the air, and before I know it — I was so full of the excitement and cheering I upped and ran away.

I find myself in the middle of nowhere but free. This is
when I have to decide — be free in nowhere or enslaved in somewhere — slave — free — slave — free. I'll make me a somewhere.

• • •

I'M BREATHING THE WATER NOW by Bash Halow

*A past-her-prime hospice worker defends her relationship to the
town's black-sheep garage mechanic.*

WOMAN
forties to fifties
dramatic

Because I'm lonely, Mr. Riley! I'm lonely! Do you understand
that? You had a wife. You had a good long marriage to her.
What do I have? I'm in my forties. My forties! And all I have
to show for it a tiny one bedroom house, that I rent, that I don't
even own for godsakes. You have children. Sure they're grown
and gone now, but still they're there. They are someone to have
Thanksgiving with, to have Christmas or maybe even to send
you a card. I have a used car and lawn full of dandelions and
what do you think it's like at Christmas time when all you get
in the mail is a blank letter that every other blank person gets
asking them for a donation to the Red Cross or to Easter Seals
or whatever the hell you call it? So he's not Mr. Perfect. He is
not a steady job holder. And yes he doesn't cut his hair and he
is not the best . . . or the better or even a good boyfriend, but
he is all I have. What do you think I'm made out of? How do
you think it is possible for me to hold, every day, the hands of
people who die and stay strong through that, to watch that and
then go home . . . to that home . . . to that life? You've seen
one death. I've seen hundreds. I sit there. I don't even help be-

cause I'm not called until all hope is gone. I just watch. Just . . . referee the last little bit. Afterwards everyone cries. They are not tears of relief. It is not put on. It is genuine, rock-bottom sadness. It is living a horrible, answerless truth. And then you know what I do? I get my coat, five years old now, and my shoulder bag and I get into my nine-year-old car and I drive home where I turn the light switch on to the living room of my rented house; where I sit in front of the television and figure out something to have for dinner. So you'll forgive me if I admit to you that I enjoy the part of my night when I hear Ted's truck pull into the driveway. Or when I'm pushing the grocery cart down the aisle and picking out food that someone else likes. Or when I'm climbing into my bed and it is warm with the heat of someone else alive and alone like me. I make twenty thousand dollars a year. I have no retirement, no insurance. I have a job that I . . . don't really even know how I fell into. And I have a boyfriend. That's what I have. And so help me God, if you try to take him away from me, I'll never speak to you again.

• • •

THE FINGER HOLE by Ty Adams

Martha, a manic depressive, has returned to New York City from a three-month disappearance and explains her cathartic journey to an unsuspecting patient waiting to see their therapist.

MARTHA
thirties to forties
dramatic

I got out of town recently. Had to. I went up to the Catskills. Had no idea where I was going . . . just pointed a finger at an ad in the newspaper and went. But all I did when I got there was think about my life back in New York, my therapy, the unfulfilling home for my anger; the anxiety-driven energy of the city; an almost Dickensian bureaucratic inertia that hangs over the struggle . . . ya need a place to take this emotional weight and I didn't go to Crunch and bond with my sweat, so therapy was my place. With Dr. Nichols was my place. He was my Crunch and together we bonded with my sweat but on that day, a coupla months ago, THAT DAY he got off on my misery . . . well, it all changed. He might as well've trained a hot white beam of light on a glass of milk and let it sit on the window sill for the afternoon. No glass of milk could take that. Ruined milk, that's what you get.

So I went up to the Catskills. Sunny Oaks. No sun. One oak. And it didn't take long for Sunny Oaks to turn into Rainy Oaks. Toward the end, the rain was so hard, it pelted the roof like baseballs. I'm sitting on the edge of my bed, crying, that wasted, self-pity crying. I was so pathetic in my effort to continue crying that I found myself trying to keep up with the rain . . . so silly, trying to cry at the pace of a hard, long, mountain rain. I so much wanted to be amazing. Do something in life, amazing. Wouldn't it be amazing if I could keep up with the rain . . . well, I wasn't amazing. I turned out to be an average crier. The rain turned out to be amazing. It completely defeated me and without pause, soothed me, consoled me, and could've seduced me that night. The next day, the rain had stopped, and I suddenly felt the courage to ask for a ride into town. The impossible had become possible. I was coming back.

• • •

LADY DAY AT EMERSON'S BAR AND GRILL
by Lanie Robertson

In a seedy Philly bar weeks before her death, the great jazz singer Billie Holiday discusses music and her mom.

BILLIE
forties
dramatic

Ain't that the truth? Jimmie gives me moonlight, don't you
Jimmy? When I need it? Jimmy, why you sit over there in the
dark for anyway? He's not mad. He's just shy. Don't want to
be seen with no jailbird. Nah, I'm kiddin'. He's all right. See,
we got this contract which says I got to sing so many songs a
night, see, and some of 'em has to be certain ones you'll want
to hear Like "Strange Fruit" and "God Bless the Child" and
all that damn shit. But I'm not like that, see. I got to sing
the way I feel. I got to sort of roam around awhile and find the
song — or more like let the song find me. That's why Jimmy's
so good. He keeps me in line and sees I sing all the numbers
I'm supposed to. Before I get too far juiced. Last year . . . no,
year before. Spring of fifty-seven I done sing all night in a little bar outside Baltimore, my ol' home town, then some horse's
butt tell me he ain't payin' nothin' because I didn't sing "God
Bless the Child" or some shit like that. An' I didn't because of
my mom, see. I wrote that damn song for her an it always make
me think of her, and that night just happen to be the same date
as the day she died an' I flat-ass couldn't sing it. In this country you'd better move on your pocketbook instead of your feel-
ins sweetheart or you're gonna find yourself way up shit's creek
without no paddle. I sung in a club in Harlem once for six or
seven hours and they told me my drinks was all they was payin'
me. But that was right after I come out of prison. An' that was-
n't even a white man did that. That's why it's so nice singin' at
Emerson's. Em's home to me. We're ol' drinkin' buddies, ain't
we, Em? He married the sweetest bitch I ever met. Next to the
Duchess. That was my mom.

• • •

MARK by Glenn Alterman

Here, Mark desperately asks his doctor for help with a problem he's facing.

MARK
any age
comic

It's crazy. I know, I know it sounds crazy! But I'll prove it, you'll see! Don't look at me like that, PLEASE, I'm not nuts! . . . Her name's Mary, Mary, and I met her at a club downtown, a few weeks ago. Was a rainy night, I was lonely, she was standing by the bar. And all I can say was that from the minute our eyes made contact, I was SMITTEN! She walked over, said hello. We danced, hardly saying a word; just deep, dark stares. Then we went back to my place, made love, and it was like NOTHING I'd ever experienced! It was like dreaming, surreal; touching, tasting, biting. Then a deep, dark sleep. When I awoke, Mary was gone. Left me a note asking me to meet her at the club that night. I felt totally drained all day, but all I could think about was Mary. Then that night, minute I met her, the same magic! And again we went back to my place, and it was even BETTER than the night before! More brutal, devouring, more delicious! I've seen her every night since. And every morning doctor, I'm more drained. She's . . . she's very dangerous, doctor. I'm afraid. When I look in the mirror in the morning, they're there; the little mementos of Mary. *(He rolls down his shirt collar.)* Here, see, see them? These little holes on my neck? I know what they are. I know what she is. I know what she's doing to me. But I was lonely, and now, now I'm not. *(Undoing the collar even more .)* Here, look, look doctor, you tell me. Go ahead, tell me if you think I'm crazy — or just crazy in love.

• • •

THE DUSTMAN by Anastasia Traina

DUSTY
late teens (can be played as old as ninety-nine)
dramatic

That's it . . . the story I want to tell you is about my brother.
My brother's horse story. I knew it was on the tip of my eye-
lash . . . May I tell my story, now?
[WILL: If you have to.]
I do, my brother. Ahem! He is also a Dustman —
[WILL: Sandman. You said he was a Sandman.]
Sandman, Dustman, it all the same. Anyway . . . he never visits more than once, and when he comes a-calling, he will take
a person up on his horse and tell them stories. He only knows
two stories . . . one that is so glorious you can't even imagine
it . . . not even in the most ambrosial of dreams . . . His stories
can be more sublime than the most tempestuous rainbow . . .
But oh, his other story, the other story is so terrifying, so
macabre . . . ahem! We won't go into that . . . His name is Old
Shut-Eye. He is not so alarming as mortals have sketched him
in all his portraits throughout the blue moon . . . Where he is
nothing but a cryptic sack of shadowy bones . . . no . . . he has
silvery hair and he wears it in a long-winded braid . . . and a
voluminous ebony cape — It is spun from the daintiest of silk-
worms . . . and, did I forget to mention his green huntsman's
tunic embroidered with gold, high boots with star-shapened
spurs, oh and a hat fashioned like a crescent moon? He's quite
a snappy dresser . . . He's also a bit of a show-off, galloping so
fast that he gives you impression that you're flying. But he does
not discriminate, he takes people both young and old . . .

• • •

ANCIENT CONTRACT by Ty Adams

Sasha Black recalls an event in her youth that shaped and molded her journey to live the life of an animal-rights activist.

SASHA
sixties or older
dramatic

I was in Wyoming. Once. Years ago, me, a young activist . . . A line was drawn in the prairie. Literally, a line drawn. The rancher had built a fence. But not just any fence. And not just any rancher; I remember him . . . Taylor Jacks. Taylor . . . The Red Rim region. Built the fence to contain his cattle. A fence stretching across a twenty-thousand-year-old migrating route for a herd of pronghorn antelope. The fence prevented the herd from reaching their natural feeding grounds. Migrating west, as they had done for thousands of years, the antelope are swift, cud-chewing animals with not enough body fat to survive winters, so they . . . they sense storms approaching and move instinctively ahead of storms. That year, they sensed the worst blizzards in Wyoming history were coming. They did what was natural. They migrated swiftly. The barbed wire was waiting. Thousands of them hit it at sixty miles per hour. They just piled up. I was sent over from San Francisco, a young gofer sent ahead to buy supplies, get a hotel room, rent a car. Shit work for the gofer. I wasn't suppose to go out to the sight. I knew that, but I was curious so I went out anyway . . . There they were . . . Their carcasses were still mangled in the wire picked clean by the scavengers. I stood there alone, staring, tears streaming down my frozen face. It was as if I was swept away by a sense of something ancient; it was as if the skulls of the antelope were embroidered, like a quilt, into the fence; and all the other antelope from twenty thousand years of migrating, had distilled themselves into this tragic moment. And that made it something you, almost, can't change. It's like a very deep voice was saying . . .

"Run along now, little girl. Be glad you survived." But I didn't run along. I hung around. I couldn't run, I was reeling. This girl was in over her little emotional head. In my young, idealistic mind, the Ancient Contract had been broken. The antelope had been betrayed. And I saw it as my job to undo the distillation; separate the past skulls from the present; and somehow, make sense of it all.

• • •

WHITE RIVER by Mary Sue Price

Minnie is tough, pioneer stock from the Missouri Ozarks. Once a beauty, she's now in her last summer and knows it. She's a former school teacher and small-town newspaper columnist. Penniless, she's living in the home of her sister and brother-in-law in the hills around Shell Knob, Missouri, where the play is set. Minnie, who drifts in and out of reality, is convinced that White River, which was dammed in 1958, is about to return. Minnie is helping her granddaughter, Jessie, hide from the sheriff. Minnie and Nora Lynn are high above a bottomless spring that once fed White River and now feeds heavily polluted Table Rock Lake. Jessie is Minnie's daughter, Nora Lynn's mother.

MINNIE
seventies to eighties
dramatic

If I was White River, I'd come back soon. And I'd wash it all away. I'd leave us all smooth as stones and clean. I'd fill up the houses of the people who came from far away to live where they don't belong. And I'd carry them all to some other place. And I'd break open the dam and carry it, too. And if my Jessie is there or in the heart of White River, I'd carry her to a place where she can rest. *(Beat.)* Honey, you're shaking all over.

[NORA LYNN: I need a drink so bad.]

If I was White River, I'd come back soon and leave them all covered up with what I know, with the soil that comes from way up north, with the knowing that this land is mine and I shape it with my wet hands and clean it with my white foam when I come pouring over the rocks.

[NORA LYNN: Mamaw, what am I gonna do?]

If I was White River, I'd cover them all and when I was through and gone and when the flood was over, the land would be rich again, the trees could see the sun, and the birds would all rest easy and my children and all the children we have lost could find their way home.

• • •

BACK COUNTY CRIMES by Lanie Robertson

In a small southern rural town a stranger confesses his crime — the crime of serial murder.

STRANGER
over thirty-five
dramatic

I never wonted to do no evil thing. All I ever wonted was to be friendly. Only trouble I ever had come from it. Bein' friendly to folks. Folks don't like you if you're friendly. I don't understand it. Don't seem natural to me. Bet you noticed it yourself, haven't you? The way they look at you like there somethin' wrong. An' only account of I spoke to 'em. Don't make sense. Folks oughta be friendly. That how it seem to me. Folks who ain't friendly, they ain't worth nothin'. They ain't worth killin', I don't figure. Anyhow, I never killed none of 'em. Not a one of 'em. But I bet I can say who did. God killed 'em. God in his almighty righteousness. That's who killed 'em. I'd wager a bet on it. It's a shame they died. It's always a shame when folks die. But lot's of folks die. Naw, I didn't kill 'em. I can swear to it. I can promise. Ever last one of 'em, all of 'em, was alive an' well when I buried 'em. But you know what? There wasn't one of 'em, none of 'em, that was the least bit friendly.

• • •

THE ROOM INSIDE THE ROOM I'M IN by Simon Fill

Joe, early twenties, talking to his childhood best friend Essie, whom he's secretly in love with and is seeing for the first time in seven years. A subway platform.

JOE
early twenties
dramatic

Your brother kills himself and what's there to say 'cept it wasn't 'cause he . . . loved anyone. Two and a half years, like two and a half days. A few months ago I started to forget a little, and I saw you inside a library. Asleep. In a quiet room. In a room inside the room I was in. I moved closer, and there was nothing. The air. And people still in their forgetfulness. And quiet. Quiet. When I looked closer, it wasn't you at all. But an old woman, like you might look old. She opened her eyes and looked at me. But she didn't know who I was. We didn't know each other. *(Beat.)* Rick's sister Amy told him she saw you in this neighborhood last week, with groceries. I needed to find you. It's incredible how boring a subway stop is for four days.

• • •

THE SUN AND THE MOON LIVE IN THE SKY
by Ellen Lewis

This play takes place in the Sea Islands of South Carolina, among the Gullah people. It's about a young girl from New York City who enters an unfamiliar world of her ancestors. She learns about her roots and hears the stories that have been passed down through the generations. In the monologue, Cudjoe, one of the members of the community, tells a story.

CUDJOE
any age
dramatic

Miss Money, she had these children and she name them all some sort of money, she had Little Money and Little Bit of Money, and Lot's a Money, the oldest name, Money.

She didn't always have these children. She was poor once. But she know children will work hard, and she will be rich, but she didn't know nothing 'bout havin' children, so she went to Miss Story. *(Imitating Miss Story.)* Miss Money, what brings you here, you wish someone made away with, turned into, snake, frog, worm, something of that order? *(Imitating Miss Money.)* Oh nothing like that, Miss Story, I wish children. *(Imitating Miss Story.)* Children, oh that's an easy one. I'll make you all the children you want — she can do that you know. Go home, you have children, but you must treat them right, or you lose them.

She says, "All right, Miss Story," and so went home. She gets home and you should have seen, she had a whole house full of children, they all ran and hugged her and even called her Mommy. *(Imitating Miss Money.)* There was More Money and Money Money Money — they were twins. A Whole Lotta of Money, Money is the oldest, and A Little Bit a Money, the youngest. Oh she enjoyed them children so . . . *(Imitating Miss*

Money.) I have More Money and Money, Money, Money — they are twins. A Whole Lotta of Money, Money is the oldest, and A Little Bit a Money, the youngest. I live on the most beautiful land of all. So we play. I throw them up in the air, toss them around, and have a good ole time. I get hungry but I don't pay that no mind. The land it will give us food. I get too hungry to work the land, so I sell a piece to feed my children. Then I sell another, and we play, then I sell another piece of land, and we play. We play and play until no more land to sell. I know — Money, she's strong and I sell her off to another's land. "That will keep us," I said. Famine knocks on the door — all around the whispers become dark. We ignore the knocks and go on playing some more. While we play, Famine shows up. I get scared. "What you want? Shooo, shoo Famine, shoo," but Famine, she just stands there. I don't know what to do, so I give her More Money, and Money Money Money the twins. Famine takes Money Money Money and More Money away, but come back and just stand there some more. I give her Money Money, she's my favorite "here take her" I say. That seems to satisfy Famine cause she leave so's I could go on playing with my Little Bit of Money. I cry and play and cry and play and cry. A Little Bit of Money will take care of me I know. Famine knocks again. This time I trick Famine and for sure get away. I say this to A Little Bit of Money. I look in the closet — I find a bottle of wine — that I save for special occasions. I put music on the radio, I set the table nice, I bring out the bottle of wine, I toast, "To your health, to your health, to your health and to your health again."

The bottle empties and Famine lay in a stupor across the table. I take a Little Bit of Money and run. We walk up the road and down the road, up the road down the road. I can't get away from the cries in the wind.

• • •

THE CAMEL SHEPHERDS by Ty Adams

Rudy, a black man, trying to console a friend about a loss, tells the story of his father, the chain thief.

RUDY
mid-thirties
dramatic

This'll be the spot. I'll put some tape down here. The microphone'll be about . . . here. And on the front row, all tha politicians, tha mayor of New Orleans, tha governor, my boss tha prison warden, all their wives, and the rows behind 'em, the rest of the prison population. But this chair, right here on tha stage . . . this is Sheriff Cody's chair. The guest of honor. Sixty-fifth birthday. The man who's done more for prisoners in the State of Louisiana than any other. The prisoner's best friend, Sheriff Cody right here. Ya-see, thirty years ago, he was a young man, the youngest sheriff ever elected in Orleans Parish. Here's what he did: he, he went out and got money from the politicians and built this gymnasium; started a prisoner's boxin' program, respected nationwide; he, he, he got more books for the prison library than any other sheriff before 'im; and he got businesses around the state to network and hire ex-cons . . . that's big; give an ex-con a job 'cause Sheriff Cody's word was behind that ex-con. Businesspeople believed him; and that's why we are gatherin' here today at a prison gymnasium to celebrate this man who has done so much for the downtrodden.

But that's not the man I know; ya-see, my relationship with Sheriff Cody goes back, way back . . . When he was elected sheriff, I was a little boy; couldn't've been mo' than six years old; I used to tap dance for pennies on the street in the French quarter, my papa worked on tha river durin' the day; we were team, my papa and me . . . a tap-dancin' duet. I'd time it just right every day to be by tha house when he'd come home from the docks; he was more tired than anything I'd ever seen; workin' on tha Mississippi was dangerous, hard work, but he loved his work and he loved that river; said that river was his best friend. That's why I couldn't understand at tha time . . .

It was a Sunday, late, and I was waitin' for Papa to come home; he was later than usual, I could tell by the sun the way it usually hit the roof across the street and cast a shade on me just 'bout the time he got home every day; only this day I'd been in the shade 'bout an hour when this dark car drives up and Sheriff Cody gets out; sounded real nice . . .

— Come along, boy, yo papa wants to see ya.

Now Papa always told me not to fight with white people, so I got in the car; we musta drove across the river down one of them long levy dirt roads; all I remember is lookin' out tha back window at tha dust flyin' up and nobody sayin' nothin' . . . just smokin' cigars. All of a sudden, we stop. One of 'em picks me up and I can see flashlights down by tha river; figured my papa's probably down there; we walk down and I'm walkin' beside the sheriff but I don't see Papa; somebody says.

— Bring him over here.

Now I hadn't been scared up 'til then when my whole face peeled off in chill after chill . . . There was my papa; all wrapped up in heavy chains and they're pullin' him outa tha river; I knew he was gone and I was glad those nice white men was helpin' me get him out; Sheriff Cody kneeled down beside me . . .

— This yo papa, boy?

Yes, sir.

— Whadaya reckon he wanted to try an swim the river for?

I don't know, sir.

— Whadaya reckon he wanted to steal that chain for?

I don't know, sir.

— Any you boys know why these nigger chain thieves wanta keep tryin' to swim this dangerous river?

Beats the hell outa me.

And I kept thinkin', that river was his friend; it wouldn't do that to him, no it wouldn't. So we're gonna put the microphone about . . . here, and as Sheriff Cody figures . . . the prisoners will come out one at a time and play their music, we got some good musicians here; and me, I'm suppose to tap dance. Sheriff Cody has said he's seen me dance and knows I'm a good hoofer and he knows I'll do my best. But I was never the hoofer my papa was . . . no, I see myself as a storyteller, and the microphone'll be about here.

• • •

CHLOE by Glenn Alterman

CHLOE
twenty-five or older
comic

(Anxious nonstop rambling.) It's all like predetermined, preordained, whatever you want to call it, Bob. Everyone knows it; ya learn it in Life 101. There are no accidents, no, none! Not even here, in small town U.S.A. We bump, melt, merge, whatever you want to call it, with people we are meant to meet, meant to meet! I believe that, I do. I mean think about it, just think about it, Bob; fact that you're here, I'm here, and we're both sitting in your car, front of my house; ready to go, night on the town, no accident, no, no, no. No mistake, none. Preordained. And I want you to know, want you to know, Bob, I was thrilled when you called last week. Thought oh my God, BOB, imagine, finally! After all these years, Bob! Not that I was sitting by the phone, no. I'm so busy these days at the library, nonstop, go, go, go; books back and forth; library lunacy. So you were really lucky to get me in, lucky I was even home. Luck, lucky, preordained. But it was certainly a surprise. I mean after all these years of seeing you at the supermarket, passing you on the street, seeing you drive by. Certainly a surprise. And now, here, the two of us, sitting in your car, waiting, waiting patiently, may I add, for you put the key in the ignition so we can go some-

where and . . . *(Looking at him.)* So why don't you start the car? Car can't start by itself. We can't go anywhere just sitting here. *(She turns to her door.)* Why'd you open my door? . . . Bob, Bob, you don't want me to leave, do you? I can't go. No Bob, no you don't understand, this is . . . This is a brand new dress! This is our first . . . ! No, you don't understand. Bob, Bobby, Robert, this has all been — preordained!

• • •

POST PUNK LIFE by Simon Fill

The opening monologue of a memory play. Jenny goes into her past and ends on two ex-boyfriends whom she loved, Ralph and Warren. The play is about the three of them. Jenny wears black. Ralph and Warren are in the background.

JENNY
early to mid-thirties
comic

(To audience.) Look. I'm just a kid, all right? I'm trying to understand some stuff I don't. I moved to New York City when I was eighteen. Greenwich Village. NYU. *(Remembers.)* That was when I still wore skirts. Before the word "pretty" had irony in it. My freshman roommate, first week, she goes, "Peach. Peach. I look best in peach." She's dead now. She lived on the Upper East Side.

So. After NYU, the typical jobs. Six years. Assistant editor. Associate. Eleven marriage proposals. First one: blond banker, twenty-four. Fuck that. Eleventh one: ran a punk club. *(Pause.)* Fuck that.

When I was an editorial assistant, I worked for a woman whose husband died a year and a half earlier. She was thirty-four. He was an editor. I never met him. He was sick before I got there.

Acute myeloid leukemia. Or was it Huntington's? A brain tumor? I don't remember. You wonder, how do I know of such things? Am I a scientific genius? The answer has a beautiful integrity of its own. *(Pause.)* I went out with a medical student.

So. I chose to work for this woman because I heard she was powerful in feminist fiction. Whatever *that* means. Every day she'd come to the office, I'd arrange her meetings with writers. This happened for three months. But I couldn't touch her message board. You see, her husband had called her every day. And her board held all his old messages. She'd kept them for a year and a half. I only remember one. *(Softly.)* "Nothing. Just called to say hi."

One morning, shortly before I became an associate, I stepped into her office. She was sitting in the window seat, crying. I asked her what was wrong. All she could say was, "Why are all the beautiful young men so sad?" *(Pause. Softly.)* "Why are all the beautiful young men so sad?" *(A beat.)* What set Ralph and Warren apart?

• • •

VIRGINS IN ASTORIA by Phil Hines

This play takes place in a laundry room in Astoria, Queens. Marvin and his mother Mary seem to be searching for answers to their lives from other tenants, including a lonely Southern woman and a gay male couple. Marvin's dog, Tito, is in the hallway waiting to be walked. When one of the gay men appears to wash clothes, Marvin begins to question him but ends up questioning himself.

MARVIN
forties
seriocomic

There's the two guys who live across from us. One white guy and a black guy. They live there together. A couple if you know what I mean? Directly across. Sometimes I see them. Funny thing happened the other night. I was having a beer at this restaurant on Steinway. So were they. The two guys, I mean. They kept looking at me and I tried not to look at them. I was by myself, you know. Which is OK but . . . . . Anyway, they almost got up to come over. I could tell but Mitch, the black guy, stopped the white guy. He didn't want to come. He must have a problem with me? Ah, hell. Who knows why but I think the black guy thinks I tried to come on to him a few weeks ago. I don't know. You know how gay guys are? They think everybody is trying to do them. I don't think the black guy told the white guy about it. What he "thought" happened. And hey — get this! Funny damn thing was that the very next morning, I come here and I see the white guy. The schoolteacher. Guess he was doing their laundry. Christ, can you believe it? His name was — Andy, I think. He started asking a lot of questions. I asked some too. Just to be friendly. I mean, we're neighbors. So what's wrong with asking a few questions, huh? And hey — get this! I find out my ma is down here about twice a week doing yoga with him! My ma? Yoga? She's over seventy! It's OK. I mean, she has her own life. I have mine but . . . Anyway, this white gay guy takes it on himself to try and "talk" with me about my life. He says I seem sad. Sad? I think he's the sad one. He says my mom is an "incredibly fascinating woman." She's "getting in touch with herself." Says it in that kind of fag way of saying it. I'm sitting on the bench in the laundry room. He sits down beside me and puts his arm around me! I mean, he seems like a nice guy but . . . Anyway, he says he knows about my big problem. Says my mom will understand. Maybe he was trying to confuse me or something? Says my mom is ready for the "big conversation." "Talk to your mom!" he starts saying. Hell, I blame those talk shows. I tell him that all I know is that my mom and me had a bad fight two days ago about Tito. She gets angry when she can't control things. Always spoiling him. He's learning from everything she does, I tell her. I can tell he's not talking about that. I can tell he means something else. Somethin' Ma musta said to him. About me.

● ● ●

NOBODY'S FLOOD by Glenn Alterman

Michael tells his brother about the moment he became aware that he had AIDS.

MICHAEL
late teens
dramatic

I kept hoping, y'know? Kept . . . But I knew, I just . . . I was losing weight, tired all the time. Mom kept saying, "Mickey, you're getting so thin. What's wrong?" Telling her it's just stress, don't worry, Ma. Telling myself it's this or that. Anything, any excuse, one after another. But then I ran out of reasons; there were no excuses left. So finally I went to the doctor. Then last night, sitting there in the waiting room — forever. Making all kinds of deals with myself. Promises, y'know. If only . . . anything . . . I'll be good. But when he came in, was walking towards me, the look in his eyes, Barry. I'll never forget. The game was over. The doctor didn't have to say a thing — I knew.

Appendix A
Sample Play Scenes Edited into Monologues

What follows are some examples of scenes edited into monologues, demonstrating how the editing is done. In some cases the edited monologue runs longer than the two minutes required for some auditions. If you want to use any of these monologues for an audition, you might need to cut them a bit more.

Original Scene from
CORNBURY, THE QUEEN'S GOVERNOR
by William M. Hoffman and Anthony Holland

Africa, formerly an African princess, is now a slave to Lord Cornbury, the transvestite English colonial governor of New York and New Jersey (1706). Africa explains to Cornbury and his wife Marie (a kleptomaniac Frenchwoman) how she came to be taken to the rude colony of New York. They are all in prison, where they are under arrest by the forces of the evil puritanical Dutch colonists. The jailor is an ancestor of the Rockefeller family, Atticus Rockefeller.

Act II, Scene Three

Debtors' prison. In the darkness the laughter ebbs. The lights come up, revealing Africa recounting a tale to Edward and Marie. Brilliant sunshine streams through the barred window, illuminating Africa.

AFRICA: As we left the village the last sound I heard was the laughter of the village maidens. I was only twelve . . . .

MARIE: Go on, *ma chère*. You entrance us.

AFRICA: I was happy and frightened — happy because the *kundala-baku (This word is to be followed by Bantu clicking sounds.)* were over, the purification rites for a virgin princess. I was frightened because I was leaving home for the first time . . .

MARIE: A sentiment I know well.

AFRICA: I was going to the kingdom of my future husband, whom I had never seen. The women had assured me that he was both handsome and brave.

MARIE: I had no such hopes *(Pointedly looking at Edward.)* — myself.

EDWARD: *Tais-toi, Marie, je voudrais entendre cette histoire fantastique.*

AFRICA: As they bore me through the forest on a palanquin, I could hear the songs of myriad birds. *(Whistles a lovely but excruciatingly difficult bird call.)* They blended with the ever more distant sounds of the village drums. My fears gave way to imaginings as the land grew foreign. Although the old women had told me what were to be my duties as first wife of a great prince, I was without experience. How would his mother greet me? What would he look like? What would it feel like?

As thus I mused I heard cries of outrage and wailing from the front of the cortège. A slave had stumbled and dropped a tray bearing ceremonial yam cakes, among our people an ill omen. My lady-in-waiting bade me drive it from my mind, for surely would the gods protect me . . . And surely she was wrong.

For upon arrival at the great river — as grand as the Hudson — we were set upon by Arab traders. Men whom I had seen smiling at my father's court now turned their angry faces toward me. My slaves fled in terror. In vain I cried in protest; I was now a slave myself.

EDWARD: Poor princess.

MARIE: *Pauvre princesse.*

AFRICA: Princess no more, nor bride, nor daughter. I was only a frightened girl enslaved to men who dealt in flesh. *(She shudders.)* The gods have mercifully released me from the memory of the deathly caravan that bore me through the desert to Tangiers. My station recognized, I was destined to be the newest acquisition of Ahmed, the Bey of Tangiers.

My shackles were removed, and I was stripped, bathed, and anointed with precious balms. The spiteful eunuchs brought me to the chambers of their master. I had not long to wait for what they had prepared me . . . *(Reliving the moment.)* He stood before me, handsome were it not for the malevolence of his eyes. He put his fingers on my lips . . . my throat . . . my nipples . . . my — between my thighs. He turned me round . . . *(Africa closes her eyes.)*

EDWARD: Don't stop!

MARIE: *Continue!*

AFRICA: *(Opening her eyes. They are wide with horror.)* I looked up. Suddenly we were not alone. Guttural sounds escaped from the Bey's contorted mouth as he was garroted by two great men. It was horrible! Months later I was to learn that Ahmed Bey was o'erthrown by a younger brother. Such is the custom of those people. His brother, having little taste for women, gave me as a gift to a merchant with whom he wished to ingratiate himself.

(Edward and Marie sigh.)

AFRICA: Served up again, and this time to a man sickly pale to my unaccustomed eyes, I was given to a stern follower of the crucified god. After drenching me with water, he mumbled some words and set me to work in his kitchen. Mercifully, Hendrik van Loon had no interest in either sex. At night he counted his gold and left me alone. The airs of my continent are not kind to people of your race. Mijnheer van Loon soon expired of a fever . . . *(She smiles.)* I found myself on a great ship, a girl of fourteen alone with forty sailors.

EDWARD: And a virgin still?

AFRICA: A virgin still . . . I was the captain's choice . . . Bound hand and foot —

EDWARD: Yes?

AFRICA: Pinioned to his bed —

MARIE: Go on.

AFRICA: Screaming for mercy till they gagged me with a spoon, I knew this time no gods would intervene. Closer came the captain, the unfamiliar odor of his race assailing my nostrils. He placed his dirty paw under my torn chemise and hoarsely whispered —

(Enter Atticus Rockefeller, leading Rip, Spinoza, and Musee — all in chains.)

ATTICUS: There's room for more in here! 'Tis not been filled up yet! *(Exit.)*

Monologue Edited from
CORNBURY, THE QUEEN'S GOVERNOR

AFRICA
ageless (eighteen to fifty)
seriocomic

As we left the village the last sound I heard was the laughter of the village maidens. I was only twelve . . . I was happy and frightened — happy because the kundala-baku were over, the purification rites for a virgin princess. I was frightened because I was leaving home for the first time. I was going to the kingdom of my future husband, whom I had never seen. The women had assured me that he was both handsome and brave. I had no such hopes myself. As they bore me through the forest on a palanquin, I could hear the songs of myriad birds. *(Whistles a lovely but excruciatingly difficult bird call.)* They blended with the ever-more-distant sounds of the village drums. My fears gave way to imaginings as the land grew foreign. Although the old women had told me what were to be my duties as first wife of a great prince, I was without experience. How would his mother greet me? What would he look like? What would it feel like? As thus I mused I heard cries of outrage and wailing from the front of the cortège. A slave had stumbled and dropped a tray bearing ceremonial yam cakes, among our people an ill omen. My lady-in-waiting bade me drive it from my mind, for surely would the gods protect me . . . And surely she was wrong. For upon arrival at the great river — as grand as the Hudson — we were set upon by Arab traders. Men whom I had seen smiling at my father's court now turned their angry faces toward me. My slaves fled in terror. In vain I cried in protest; I was now a slave myself. Princess no more, nor bride, nor daughter. I was only a frightened girl enslaved to men who dealt in flesh. *(She shudders.)* The gods have mercifully released me from the memory of the deathly caravan that bore me through the desert to Tangiers. My station recognized, I was destined to be the newest acquisition of Ahmed, the Bey of Tangiers. My shackles were removed, and I was stripped, bathed, and anointed with precious balms. The spiteful eunuchs brought me to the chambers of their master. I had not long to wait for what they had prepared me . . . *(Reliving the moment.)* He stood before me, handsome were it not for the malevolence of his eyes. He put his fingers on my lips . . . my throat . . . my nipples . . . my — between my thighs. He turned me round . . . *(Closes her eyes, then opening them wide with horror.)* I looked up. Suddenly we were not alone. Guttural sounds escaped from the Bey's contorted mouth as he was garroted by two great men. It was horrible! Months later I was to learn that Ahmed Bey was o'erthrown by a younger brother. Such is the custom of those people. His brother, having little taste for women, gave me as a gift to a merchant with whom he wished to ingratiate himself. Served up again, and this time to a man sickly pale to my unaccustomed eyes, I was given to a stern follower of the crucified god. After drenching me with water, he mumbled some words and set me to work in his kitchen. Mercifully, Hendrik van Loon had no interest in either sex. At night he counted his gold and left me alone. The airs of my continent are not kind to people of your race. Mijnheer van Loon soon expired of a fever . . . *(She smiles.)* I found myself on a great ship, a girl of fourteen alone with forty sailors. A virgin still . . . I was the captain's choice . . . Bound hand and foot — Pinioned to his bed — Screaming for mercy till they gagged me with a spoon, I knew this time no gods would intervene. Closer came the captain, the unfamiliar odor of his race assailing my nostrils.

DISCUSSION OF MONOLOGUE EDITED FROM *CORNBURY, THE QUEEN'S GOVERNOR*

For the most part, all that was required here was editing out the dialogue of the other characters in the scene. Africa's story was the basis of the scene and the monologue. There are many plays where editing scenes such as this one into a monologue are relatively simple. Although this is a memory monologue, the images and emotions are so powerful it can be used as an audition monologue. Because of the subject matter (and powerful descriptions), you'll need to be discerning as to where and for whom you'll use this type of material.

• • •

Original Scene from
MERMAIDS ON THE HUDSON by Anastasia Traina

India sits alone underneath the George Washington Bridge. We hear the lapping of waves against cold rocks. The lights palely shimmer from the bridge as the sun sets. Jake, a young man, wearing a red jacket, sneaks up on India, his old childhood sweetheart and best friend, to wish her happy birthday. He quietly turns away for a second and lights a lighter.

JAKE: *(Softly.)* Happy birthday to . . .
   (India jumps from fright.)
JAKE: you. Hello stranger —
INDIA: You . . . scared me.
   (Jake kneels down next to India.)
JAKE: Happy birthday . . . to you —
INDIA: I hate that song.
(Jake blows out the lighter.)
JAKE: Wow, it's your birthday. How old are you now?
INDIA: I forget.
   (Jake sits.)
JAKE: Sorry I'm late.
INDIA: I don't remember inviting you.
JAKE: But you knew I'd be here . . .
   (India's eyes glaze over. Jake gets lost in his castle-building.)
JAKE: My Mom went to the doctor 'cause she was seeing these white spots and they would . . . well, she said that they were growing tails —
INDIA: Tails?
JAKE: Yeah, tails . . . you know like little monkeys' tails —
INDIA: Monkey tails? Not dogs' tails —
JAKE: Well now let me think, they could've been dogs' tails . . . now that's an interesting question, I never really asked her what the tails looked like exactly —
   (Jake quickly leans over and tries to kiss India. India pulls away.)

INDIA: I don't kiss people.

JAKE: Oh?

INDIA: Anymore.

JAKE: I just thought . . .

INDIA: Yes, well . . .

JAKE: I like it when the bridge is all lit up like that. It's so monumental looking against the night sky — Like old memories . . .

INDIA: Yeah. Not all memories are worth remembering . . . yeah.

(Jake looks searchingly at India.)

INDIA: It's cold out here.

(Jake takes off his hat and hands it to India.)

JAKE: Here . . . take my hat.

INDIA: No, really, it's OK.

JAKE: I'm not cold. Go on, take it . . .

(India takes the hat and puts it on.)

INDIA: Thanks.

JAKE: Better?

INDIA: Much.

(They stare out into the river.)

JAKE: My mom told the doctor that those little white spots were penetrating her skin . . . she thought it was some kind of biological warfare that our next door neighbor was experimenting with . . . and do you know what that doctor asked her? He asked her what kind of drugs she was on. I can't believe it, now he's supposed be a good doctor, a real big shot, specializing in female troubles between the ages of forty and fifty. She saw him on television and everything, I think it was the Phil Donohue show . . . Now my mom is like tangled up in her own terror . . . I'm just chattering on here, I guess, I'm nervous, that's what happens when I'm nervous, I just chatter on and on and on. I've never really done this before . . . usually I don't get to . . . I don't talk about the intimate details of my life with a complete stranger . . . I mean it feels kind of weird . . . Hello stranger.

INDIA: I'm not a stranger. Stop saying that.

JAKE: You've been acting like one.

INDIA: I don't know what your talking about.

JAKE: Oh I think you do. It took a lot a work to contact you again.

Monologue Edited from
MERMAIDS ON THE HUDSON

JAKE
eighteen to fifty
seriocomic

(Softly.) Happy birthday to . . . you . . . Hello stranger — Happy birthday . . . to you — Sorry I'm late . . . But you knew I'd be here. My Mom went to the doctor 'cause she was seeing these white spots and they would . . . well, she said that they were growing tails — Yeah, tails . . . you know like little monkeys' tails . . . Well now let me think, they could've been dogs' tails. I never really asked her what the tails looked like exactly. I like it when the bridge is all lit up like that. It's so monumental look-ing against the night sky — Like old memories . . . My Mom told the doctor that those little white spots were penetrating her skin. She thought it was some kind of biological warfare that our next-door neighbor was experimenting with . . . and do you know what that doctor asked her? He asked her what kind of drugs she was on. I can't believe it, now he's supposed be a good doctor, a real big shot, specializing in female troubles between the ages of forty and fifty. She saw him on television and every-thing, I think it was the Phil Donohue show . . . Now my mom is like tangled up in her own terror . . . I'm just chattering on here, I guess, I'm nervous, that's what happens when I'm nerv-ous, I just chatter on and on and on. I've never really done this before . . . usually I don't get to . . . I don't talk about the in-timate details of my life with a complete stranger . . . I mean it feels kind of weird . . . Hello stranger.

Again, all that was required here was cutting the other character's dialogue. You'll find that editing two character scenes into monologues are generally easier than scenes with multiple characters. You'll notice that in the scene version there are a lot of stage directions. You must decide if the stage directions in the play will be of any use to you for an audition monologue. If the stage directions are not useful, then you'll have to find a creative way to keep the feel of the stage direction without including them. In some plays the stage directions can be so specific to the play, and so intrinsic to the scene that it will make the transition to audition monologue impossible. In the case of *Mermaids on the Hudson*, this wasn't a problem. Also, If you'll notice, some of the unnecessary expositional material was cut when creating the monologue.

• • •

Original Scene from
WILD ECHINACEA by Jonathan Reuning

Echinacea Fields, a young woman with a long history of short marriages, makes the acquaintance of her next-door neighbor, Keith Honeydew, the most relationship-challenged single man in all of recorded suburbia.

Act I, Scene One

Lights up. It's spring. The suburbs. A sunny day. A driveway leading upstage to a small garage with a shingled roof. A basketball hoop and backboard mounted centrally above the garage door. The back end of a vintage Plymouth automobile jetted out from a downstage wing. Keith, dressed in an old V-neck

T-shirt, double-knit pants, basketball sneakers, and a whistle around his neck, enters bouncing a basketball. He drives toward the basket, shoots a lay-up, misses, and continues to miss as he practices. Echinacea, in bedclothes and bathrobe, enters downstage. A pair of blue jeans are draped across her shoulder.)

ECHINACEA: Excuse me.

KEITH: Just a moment.

ECHINACEA: I'm sorry, but I've just had an altercation with my husband, and have spent the past twenty minutes stripping the house of everything that smells of him. I happened to catch a glimpse of you from my kitchen window and noticed the shabby state of your trousers. I thought maybe this pair of Levi's would provide you some relief.

KEITH: That's very thoughtful, but don't you see how your endless meddling is ruining my life?

ECHINACEA: I see I've come at a bad time. *(Begins to leave.)*

KEITH: *(Briefly puts on a pair of eyeglasses.)* Wait a minute. I'm sorry. I thought you were my mother. *(Removes his glasses and back-pockets them.)*

ECHINACEA: I beg your pardon?

KEITH: It was the bathrobe in the middle of the day.

ECHINACEA: Forgive my appearance, I —

KEITH: No, no. I'm sure you're very comfortable.

ECHINACEA: I've had quieter mornings. Perhaps you heard the gunfire? Anyway, I don't want to keep you. My ambulance should be arriving any —

(Echinacea collapses in his arms, her bathrobe opens revealing a bandaged wound to her side. A pastel billow of pink where blood has escaped. Keith speaks as he lowers her to the ground and positions her head on his lap.)

KEITH: Goodness. Please, make yourself comfortable.

ECHINACEA: I'm sorry to just drop by.

KEITH: Not at all.

ECHINACEA: The Levis are only slightly faded.

KEITH: You're very kind to think of me at such a time. Who are you?

ECHINACEA: Oh I'm sorry. I'm your next-door neighbor, Echinacea. Echinacea Fields.

KEITH: Pleased to meet you. Welcome to the neighborhood.

ECHINACEA: Actually, I've lived here all my life.

KEITH: You don't say?

ECHINACEA: I meant to introduce myself earlier, but things have been hectic . . .

KEITH: No need to apologize, that's a nasty looking wound.

ECHINACEA: I'm trying not to dwell on it, but I'd fully understand if you complained about the noise.

KEITH: Somehow this doesn't seem the time.

ECHINACEA: I'm not sure when you'll be able to catch me again.

KEITH: I've been meaning to have a word with you. Lately it seems —

ECHINACEA: You're kind to be so brief. I hope now this is behind us. My soon-to-be ex-husband claimed he was trying to shoot the cable box off our television set. The shriek of agony, of course, belonged to me.

KEITH: I only heard the gunfire.

ECHINACEA: I hope you're not just saying that.

KEITH: It broke the concentration of my cheerleaders. They ran screaming from the driveway.

ECHINACEA: I assure you the commotion will stop. I'll never marry again.

KEITH: However you'd like to arrange it. But where are my manners? Is there anything you'd like to borrow?

ECHINACEA: I'm all compressed and cauterized so there really isn't a thing. Actually, your mere presence is helping me concentrate on living.

KEITH: As long as I'm not keeping you.

ECHINACEA: Not at all. I'd be most grateful, however, if you tried to modulate your voice in an interesting way. I've noticed that it's rather monotone, and I'm afraid my chances of survival are slim if you bore me.

KEITH: Oh good Lord.

ECHINACEA: I know from experience I'm susceptible to shock. If you notice me starting to drift, I'd be grateful if you made me aware of it.

KEITH: You're sure you wouldn't rather I drove you to the hospital?

ECHINACEA: I don't feel at this stage I shouldn't be moved by anyone other than a professional. But if my eyes close, I'd appreciate a pinch.

KEITH: As I've said, my pantry is your pantry.

ECHINACEA: That's most reassuring, but what I mean is, you can pinch me.

KEITH: Pinch you?

ECHINACEA: On the arm would be fine.

(He pinches her on the arm.)

ECHINACEA: Ouch!

KEITH: Sorry!

ECHINACEA: No, excellent. Just like that, if you see my eyes close.

KEITH: Are you sure now?

ECHINACEA: Absolutely. And as an added precaution, we should probably keep talking. You said something earlier I allowed to go unexamined. *(Raises her hand)*

KEITH: Is there a question?

ECHINACEA: Yes. *(Lowers her hand)* Are they very, very small?

KEITH: I beg your pardon?

ECHINACEA: You mentioned cheerleaders. I don't recall ever seeing one on your driveway.

KEITH: They're average height, I suppose, but very thin, or at least that's how I imagine them. *(Pinches her.)*

ECHINACEA: Ouch!

KEITH: Too hard?

ECHINACEA: The pressure was perfect, but that was just a blink.

KEITH: Of course. I'm so sorry.

ECHINACEA: That's all right. I'm glad you're paying attention.

KEITH: Do you think, ideally then, I should pay less attention?

ECHINACEA: We're not trying to split hairs here, um . . .

KEITH: Keith.

ECHINACEA: Right.

KEITH: Honeydew.

ECHINACEA: Huh huh, so if I blink, no pinch. If I fall into some type of coma — I'm sorry, is this going to be hard for you?

KEITH: No, no, I'm just . . .

ECHINACEA: Confused?

KEITH: Yes.

ECHINACEA: Don't sweat it. The sun, the dust, the powder burns — I'm sure I'm blinking much longer than normal.

KEITH: OK, so there's no misunderstanding — when you say blink . . .

ECHINACEA: When I say blink?

KEITH: when you say blink . . .

ECHINACEA: Nothing when I say blink.

KEITH: So your eyes won't necessarily close?

ECHINACEA: Oh come on now.

KEITH: Now?

ECHINACEA: Coma. *(He pinches her.)* Ouch! I can't believe you did that.

KEITH: Sorry!

ECHINACEA: I said coma.

KEITH: You said coma.

ECHINACEA: I said coma!

KEITH: So when you say coma, you don't mean coma?

ECHINACEA: If I say coma I can't be in a coma, can I?

KEITH: Of course not. What will you say, then?

ECHINACEA: I won't be able to say anything. No verbal signal. Nothing.

KEITH: Nothing.

ECHINACEA: Not a word.

KEITH: Got it. Wow. Scary . . . are you sure there isn't anything . . .

ECHINACEA: I'm all set on dry goods, thank you . . .

KEITH: Keith.

ECHINACEA: Uh huh.

KEITH: Honeydew.

ECHINACEA: No melon either, thanks. So I'm going to try resting with my eyes open, interspersed with occasional blinks. All I need you to do is wave down the ambulance, if and when it ever — *(She falls into coma.)*

Monologue Edited from
WILD ECHINACEA

Echinacea, in bedclothes and bathrobe, enters downstage. A pair of blue jeans are draped across her shoulder.

ECHINACEA
twenty
darkly comic

Excuse me. I'm sorry, but I've just had an altercation with my husband, and have spent the past twenty minutes stripping the house of everything that smells of him. I happened to catch a glimpse of you from my kitchen window and noticed the shabby state of your trousers. I thought maybe this pair of Levi's would provide you some relief . . . I beg your pardon? Forgive my appearance, I — I've had quieter mornings. Perhaps you heard the gunfire? Anyway, I don't want to keep you. My ambulance should be arriving any — *(She collapses, her bathrobe opens revealing a bandaged wound to her side. [Note: This action will be difficult to perform at an audition. You'll have to discover an action that is playable for an audition monologue.])* I'm sorry to just drop by. The Levi's are only slightly faded . . . I'm your next-door neighbor, Echinacea. Echinacea Fields. I meant to introduce myself earlier, but things have been hectic. My soon-to-be ex-husband claimed he was trying to shoot the cable box off our television set. The shriek of agony, of course, belonged to me. I'd fully understand if you complained about the noise [but] I assure you the commotion will stop. I'll never marry again . . . I'm all compressed and cauterized so there really isn't a thing — Actually, your mere presence is helping me concentrate on living. I'd be most grateful, however, if you tried to modulate your voice in an interesting way. I've noticed that it's rather monotone and I'm afraid my chances of survival are slim if you bore me . . . I don't feel at this stage I shouldn't be moved by anyone other than a professional, but if my eyes close, I'd appreciate a pinch . . . On the arm would be fine.

DISCUSSION OF MONOLOGUE EDITED FROM
WILD ECHINACEA

Here again we have a two-character scene. All that was required was deleting the other character's dialogue. Scenes where two characters are meeting for the first time can work well for the audition monologue. One character quite often is telling the other character about himself and his life while the other character is mainly listening; a perfect setup for a monologue. If there is too much exposition and not enough action then the scene won't work well for auditions. You'll notice that in the scene, at different times there is repetition in the dialogue. Although it's effective in the dialogue, generally it won't be of any use when edited into a monologue.

The monologue ends after Keith pinches Echinacea. Once one character physically interacts with the other character in a scene (in this case, pinching), and the (pinched) character must respond, it will be difficult to play the reactive dialogue that follows. One thing to notice is that this is very clearly a "character monologue." The material doesn't have much conflict in it. This monologue might be appropriate for certain plays where there are characters similar to Echinacea.

• • •

Original Scene from
BUM A SHOT by Michael Bettencourt

Steel Eye is a vagrant, female, age hard to determine but certainly a veteran of the streets. Ronald Bitters is a tourist with a camera. They are in a major American city; the weather is cold. Steel Eye is out trolling for change. She has a coffee can at her feet. As she begins speaking, she will acknowledge the contributions of people. Halfway through her first spiel, Bitters enters, camera around his neck. It's not an expensive camera — something like a Pentax K-1000 or a point-and-shoot — and he's taking tourist photos.

STEEL EYE: Practice your Catholic charity, Muslim piety, Sufi mysticism, Buddhist mindfulness, Lutheran — whatever you do — thank you — drop some dough in my can below. — Praise be! — I don't take contributions from United Way, Amway, the Eightfold Way, or curds and whey. I just hit the highway, the byway, and do it my way. — Much appreciated. — No middle man here, no overhead — all funds expended directly for recipients. — Thanks. — Help me make it through the night — and day. Just do it.

(Bitters takes a picture of Steel Eye prepares to move on.)

STEEL EYE: Hey, what do you think you're doing?

BITTERS: What?

STEEL EYE: What do you think you're doing?

BITTERS: Taking pictures.

STEEL EYE: No, no, no, no, no. Stand to one side for a second.

(Bitters hesitates, clearly uncomfortable.)

STEEL EYE: Stand over here. We have to talk. Just watch.

(Bitters stands to one side.)

STEEL EYE: *(Back to her spiel, with asides to Bitters. To crowd.)* Charity begins at home — my home. Which you're walking on. Make these mean streets sweeter. — Have a nice day, too. — *(To Bitters.)* I have to work the lunch crowd here, best money during the day. Rush hour sucks — everyone's like a razor through butter. *(To crowd, in rhythm.)* I'm a refugee in a democracy — there is no lunch that's free for me. Make sure I have my balanced nutrition. *(To Bitters.)* What's your name?

BITTERS: Ronald Bitters.

STEEL EYE: Well, Roland —

BITTERS: Ronald.

STEEL EYE: What's a couple of letters? — Thanks for the pennies. — *(To crowd.)* Legal tender makes me tender. Render some tender here. Money may not buy happiness — but poverty sucks. Some march for dimes — I sashay for quarters. — Thanks. — *(To Bitters.)* Roland —

BITTERS: Ronald.

STEEL EYE: Daffy. If you're going to be picky about a couple of letters, then it's Daffy. You are seeing an artist in action, Daffy. Consummate. *(To crowd.)* If money grew on trees, poor people wouldn't have axes. I don't want your social change, just your spare change. — Gracias. Gracias. — Don't give me your tired, your poor, your hoodoo masses — just *(Breaks into rendition of last phrase of the Beatles' cover of "Money.")* money / That's what I want.

Money makes my world go around. Make it turn faster. — Bottom of the day to you. — *(Looks up and down the street and sees a break in the action.)* Almost one o'clock. Force-fed, they scoot back to their cubicles. *(Picks up the can, inspects the contents.)* Daffy, there is an endless stream of cash on the hoof here. They're going to part with it some place, so why not here. I give them a little performance, they feel I've earned their money. It's no different than what they do over in the theater district. Now, you. Give me that film.

BITTERS: What?

STEEL EYE: Really deaf, or just convenient deaf? Give me the film.

BITTERS: Why?

STEEL EYE: You have my picture on it. I'm copyrighted.

BITTERS: No, you're not.

STEEL EYE: *(Makes a C with her hand on her forehead.)* If I say I am, I am. Now, give me the film or give me ten dollars.

BITTERS: Ten dollars?

STEEL EYE: Don't you bring *any* original conversation to the table? *(Empties the can and puts it back down.)* My face is my property. You took my property. So you either pay me for what you took or give me the film.

BITTERS: You're just part of the street.

STEEL EYE: Yeah?

BITTERS: I was taking a picture of that building over there —

STEEL EYE: Oh, really? That lovely anonymous heap of chrome and crap —

BITTERS: — you just happened to be in the picture —

STEEL EYE: — is *so* overphotographed —

BITTERS: — and you were right there —

STEEL EYE: — I just have to shoo them away —

BITTERS: — so the picture wasn't about you —

STEEL EYE: — the photographers get so thick around here — *(Pause.)* And you still want to maintain that I just "happened" to be in the picture?

BITTERS: Yes. *(Longish pause, can't meet her eyes.)* So I don't owe you anything.

STEEL EYE: I'm going to assume by that pause that you are too honest a man to lie very well. Just wait. *(To the crowd.)* Shekels, lira, marks, pounds — we take it all. We're multi-denominational here. Money is the root of all evil — give me a chance to go to hell. *(Pause.)* Petered out. I shouldn't have been talking to you. Oh well, enough for a hot and a cot.

(Turns to Bitters. In these following lines, Bitters can barely get his responses in.)

STEEL EYE: Now, like I said, I'm going to assume honesty on your part because you really don't have enough poker in your face to make a lie stick. So, since I, and not the building, was the subject of your clickery, I want the film — or the sawbuck. I'd ask for the camera, but it's a piece of dreck. Ding! You've had enough time to consider.

BITTERS: I'm late. I have to meet —

STEEL EYE: You don't get it, do you? This is not a polite request. You stole something from me.

BITTERS: Look, I'm just here for the day.

STEEL EYE: Day tripper, in for a show and a nice place to go. Come hear a tune and then back to the cocoon.

BITTERS: Please, I have to go —

STEEL EYE: The film or a tenner — which will it be?

BITTERS: I can't give you the film.

STEEL EYE: Yes, that film must have those deathless photos of the missus in front of the fountain, the missus in front of the peep show, the missus —

BITTERS: Five dollars.

STEEL EYE: Ten — the going rate for street-level intellectual property.

(Bitters looks around, as if for a police officer.)

STEEL EYE: Look, you're free to go if you want. I can't force you to own up to your responsibilities. But let me ask you this, Daffy, before you scoot, before you abdicate: what do you do for work in your cocoon?

BITTERS: I'm an accountant.

STEEL EYE: Hmm. And if the books don't balance — Work with me here, Daffy.

BITTERS: I have to balance them.

STEEL EYE: Which means you're in the honesty business, right? Right?

BITTERS: Right.

STEEL EYE: If you dive away with the money, you'll never in-voice in this town again — correct?

BITTERS: Yes.

STEEL EYE: Consider yourself an honest man?

BITTERS: Yes.

STEEL EYE: So what's the problem here, Daffy? If I paint a picture, if I write a book — let's say an accounting textbook! — and I sell it, I get paid for the product, right?

BITTERS: Right.

STEEL EYE: This face — the textbook of a lifetime. Some people put faces on canvas; I paste it on my bones. Just a different way to stretch it. Look at it, Daffy, look at it closely. Have you ever been this close to a street person before, Daffy? Sensually speaking? All senses hooked? Look. Closely.

(Bitters looks.)

STEEL EYE: The work of a lifetime, right? Like a map, huh? See, your skin is smooth — floppy wattles, to be sure, the result of too much laxness in your own life — but mine — like deltas, escarpments, faults, exfoliations. A whole life inscribed here. My property.

BITTERS: Um —

STEEL EYE: A fullness, a combustionary complexity —

BITTERS: Please —

STEEL EYE: Can you truthfully say you aren't you the least bit interested?

BITTERS: *(Getting defensive.)* Look — !!

STEEL EYE: That's all I'm asking you to do. When you took your picture, Daffy, were you thinking, "She has the face that launched a thousand quips" and not only do I want to know about it, I will pay the price for the knowledge?

BITTERS: You don't have the right —

STEEL EYE: I'll spare you the embarrassment of lying again: No, you weren't, Daffy. You told yourself you were just taking a picture of a "street scene," a *thing*. But it's my face that made the whole *thing* interest you in the first place. Created after a lifetime of debauch and redemption, riches and rags, tastes great/less filling — you were drawn to it, even if you won't admit it.

BITTERS: I'm leaving.

STEEL EYE: Before you do, answer me one question: Do I not bleed, Daffy?

BITTERS: Theoretically.

STEEL EYE: Two more. Do I not have — urges, artistic and otherwise, like you?

BITTERS: Well —

STEEL EYE: Last one. Aren't you and I, really, kin under the skin?

BITTERS: Not really —

STEEL EYE: So with peace in your heart you can cut our common tether to protect some lousy film with pictures on it you'll never look at more than once, or a ten-spot you're going to waste on some street-vendor sweatshirt that will unthread in the first wash. I am insulted and made *de trop* by your betrayal. So, pay up now.

BITTERS: I won't.

STEEL EYE: Then reap the whirlwind. I'm calling a cop.

BITTERS: For what?

STEEL EYE: Theft. I told you — my face is my commodity.

BITTERS: I'm leaving.

STEEL EYE: *(Picks up her can and says in a very loud but measured tone.)* Help. Help. his man is trying to steal my money. Someone save me.

BITTERS: Stop this!

STEEL EYE: *(In a whisper.)* Only you can stop this. *(Loudly.)* Help. Help. Damsel in distress, right here.

BITTERS: All right! Enough. Put it down. I said five dollars. I'll pay five dollars.

STEEL EYE: Ten the minimum bid. Help.

BITTERS: Five. I only have five on me.

STEEL EYE: Oh, doing that city *thang*, not a lot of cash in your pockets. Sad, but wise. *(Goes to say "Help" again to get Bitters to respond, then stops.)* OK, five dollars. But you have to work off your debt.

BITTERS: My debt?

STEEL EYE: The rump five dollars. I'd prefer money, of course, since good will buys no food, but we can work something out. First, the fiver.

BITTERS: *(Hands her five dollars.)* I can't believe —

STEEL EYE: A man of honor. Now, Daffy, stand right here. *(She leans the two signs against him and puts the can on the ground.)* OK, earn me fifty cents. *(She backs off slightly, then speaks as if to a passerby.)* It's a student film project. Oops, you had a chance right there. Too late.

BITTERS: I can't do this.

STEEL EYE: C'mon, begging's not hard. Just use a little style, a little of that panache lurking beneath your wobbly wattles. Just fifty cents, two measly heads of Washington. Then your debt is paid.

BITTERS: I can't.

STEEL EYE: Jeez, the quality of the help these days! All right, Daffy, I'll make it easy for you. *(Walks up closely to him.)* Convince *me* to give you two quarters. *(Takes two coins from her pocket.)* Starting now.

BITTERS: I'm hungry —

STEEL EYE: I don't think so.

BITTERS: I *am* hungry, and I need a place to stay tonight. Won't you give me some money?

STEEL EYE: OK, OK, bricks are made from mud. We can work with this. A performance review: Didn't convince me — why? So what. Lots of hungry and homeless people around — a dime for a double dozen. Go get a job — lazy, worthless bum. No, your average turista — like this guy I met one time — Daffy, I think his name was — is not moved by simple want or blatant need. They require a return on investment. So beggars need an angle, a hook, a shtick. I got mine. What's yours?

BITTERS: I don't have an angle.

STEEL EYE: This is getting to be a long afternoon. Do you have any idea what I'm talking about?

BITTERS: I have money at the hotel. I'll come back —

STEEL EYE: But you're so close! C'mon, one more try. I know you have it in you, somewhere in that fatted-calf body of yours. A little force, a little — *sizzle*, a little *show biz*.
(Bitters looks like he's concentrating mightily, then he bursts

into a clownish rendition of a bit of doggerel: spastic soft shoe, e.g.)

BITTERS: "I don't care if it's a nickel or a dime / I'll take the money if you'll take the time."

(Steel Eye looks at him with what looks like admiration.)

STEEL EYE: Bravo, Herr Daffy. Bravo. *(Takes out two quarters and hands them to Bitters.)* Now I *know* that I have spent my money well for I have been entertained by the masses. I can put the cocoon back on and off I go. Bravo. *(Steel Eye bundles up her things.)* You are released. I have to go to my late afternoon location. Enjoy the picture.

(Bitters stands there confused.)

STEEL EYE: What?

BITTERS: I'm sorry.

STEEL EYE: For what? *(Steps close to him.)* This face? This face was once where you were. It doesn't take much. It doesn't take much at all. Dismissed.

(Bitters leaves.)

STEEL EYE: Oh, life in the city can be so *interesting*! Now he'll have quite the story to tell when he goes into the orifice on Monday. He survived the urban arcade. *(Picks up her belongings.)* I only hope the same can be said for all of us.

(Steel Eye leaves, carting off her materials. Blackout.)

Monologue Edited from
BUM A SHOT

STEEL EYE
indeterminate age
seriocomic

Practice your Catholic charity, Muslim piety, Sufi mysticism, Buddhist mindfulness, Lutheran — whatever you do — thank you — drop some dough in my can below. All funds expended directly for recipients. Hey, hey, hey — what'd'ya think you're doing? No, no, no, no, no. Give me that film, or give me ten dollars — or my face — my face is property. This face is copyrighted. You take a picture, you take my property. Oh, this is news to you? Well, look — look at it closely. The work of a lifetime, pasted on my bones. "The face that launched a thousand quips." And no suburban turista is going to steal it. Hey! Hey!! All right, that's it — I'm calling me a cop. You brought this on yourself. (*In a falsely "damsel" voice.*) "This man is trying to steal my money." Sorry, you forced it on me. "Damsel in distress here" — stop doing that! — "Someone save me." I take it your hand-flapping means "negotiate." Tutorial, then: Do I not bleed? Even you can't disagree with that. And (*pointing to face*) really, kin under the skin, aren't we? Tough to swallow that? Look again. This face — was once where you were. Really. It doesn't take much. It doesn't take much at all. Actually, looking at you looking like you do — I don't want your money. Tainted, wouldn't it be, if I took it? The film? On the house. So, go on — go on. Dismissed. (*The tourist hands Steel Eye money.*) Well, thanks. (*She watches the tourist walk off.*) Twenty! That shtick *always* works. It's my best. And a story for him at the orifice on Monday. Survived the urban arcade. I only hope on Monday the same can be said for all of us.

DISCUSSION OF MONOLOGUE EDITED FROM *BUM A SHOT*

Here is a short, two-person one-act play in which the other character's dialogue in the play is eliminated. The scene is so specifically directed at the other character that turning it into a monologue (with a few line adjustments) was relatively simple. Obviously in a play of this length, there will be to be some judicious editing. As always, keep only the dialogue that is necessary to make the story clear and to give you something to play at an audition.

• • •

Original Scene from
SHEPHERD'S BUSH by Scott C. Sickles

Foster and Ackerley are outside the Brunswick Square flat in England.

ACKERLEY: I couldn't help being effusive. She was marvelous. You were afraid she'd be some graffiti-ed hussy.

FORSTER: I *wanted* her to be a graffiti-ed hussy! Then I could have felt superior and insulted her with witticisms she didn't understand. No, this woman understands everything! Not to mention the proprietary screams at Bob! It's as though she owns him!

ACKERLEY: And we must never forget you're his true and rightful owner, right?

FORSTER: You don't understand, Joe. What if he marries her?

ACKERLEY: You've carried on with married men before. Hell, you've supported their families.

FORSTER: I didn't wait over half a century to find I wanted to live the rest of my days with any of *them*! (Pause) Oh, to hell with it. Would you like to come in or . . .

(Forster and Ackerley see Bob enter from the edge of the walkway.)

BOB: Good evening, gentlemen.

ACKERLEY: Bob. You're here. It's late. I must be going.

FORSTER: Must you? Surely, you can stay for a spot of tea or . . . bourbon or . . .

ACKERLEY: I'll call you both about the show. And Bob. I can't tell you how charming I find your May.

FORSTER: Perhaps, you should go.

ACKERLEY: She's more than a lady; she's an honest-to-God woman. A rarity, I must say.

FORSTER: I think I hear Queenie pining for you.

ACKERLEY: In fact, she may be the only one.

BOB: That's very kind of you, Joe.

FORSTER: Too kind. Good night.

ACKERLEY: Good night, gentlemen. "Parting is such sweet" et cetera, et cetera. *(Exits.)*

FORSTER: *(Pause.)* Yes?

BOB: I . . . I wanted to . . .

FORSTER: Be careful how you finish that sentence, Mr. Buckingham.

BOB: What am I supposed to do, Morgan? I am an officer of the law. You of all people know how it would look if you and I had —

FORSTER: So you're saying this woman is a mask? She exists to make you appear acceptable to the world and you have no feelings for her. Is that it?

BOB: I don't know what I feel for her.

FORSTER: Yes, you do. You just can't say it to my face. You're charmed by her. She gives you respectability you don't think you have otherwise. But don't try to spare my feelings by saying she's only here for appearances. I watched you tonight. You were not being merely charming with her. You were affectionate, tender, even loving. You were able to treat her publicly the exact same way you treat me privately. You must have felt quite relieved.

BOB: All right, yes I admire her. I am . . . developing feelings for her. I may even someday love her. I thought love was a good thing. Everyone's always complaining there isn't enough of it in the world. For God's sake, Morgan, when did caring about people and wanting to make them happy become a sin? Look, I don't know how to explain it to you. I should go.

FORSTER: Give the lady my regards. That's is where you're off to, isn't it?

BOB: I'm going home.

FORSTER: It's a pity that's not here.

BOB: Morgan. Are you all right?

FORSTER: I am tired and I am old. If I appeared tense or anxious this evening, that is why. I am pleased you found someone so . . . like she is. In fact, why aren't you going to her?

BOB: It's late.

FORSTER: I see. She's not that kind of girl then who would . . .
BOB: She most certainly is not!
FORSTER: But, I am? *(Pause.)* Go home, Bob.

Monologue Edited from
SHEPHERD'S BUSH

FORSTER
fifty-two
dramatic

I know, Bob. You're an officer of the law and I of all people know how it would look if . . . And you say this woman is a mask? She exists to make you appear acceptable to the world and you have no feelings for her. Is that it? We both know that's not true; you just can't say it to my face! You're charmed by her. She gives you respectability you don't think you have otherwise. But don't try to spare my feelings by saying she's only here for appearances. I watched you tonight. You were not being merely charming with her. You were affectionate, tender, even loving. You were able to treat her publicly the exact same way you treat me privately. You must have felt quite relieved. I apologize. Robert. I am tired and I am old. If I appeared tense or anxious this evening, that is why. I am pleased you found someone so . . . like she is. You should go. Give the lady my regards. That is where you're off to, isn't it? Go home, Bob.

DISCUSSION OF MONOLOGUE EDITED FROM
SHEPHERD'S BUSH

The first part of this scene gives us some background information about several of the characters in the play. It doesn't offer us much material that can be useful for an audition monologue. It is for that reason that that the material in that section is not used in the monologue.

The later part of the scene (Forster's scene and dialogue with Bob) gives us the most substantial material for an actable audition monologue. The dialogue is more direct (to Bob) and playable for solo material. That part of the scene also includes characters with conflicts that we can use in the monologue.

• • •

Original Scene from
RED TIDE BLOOMING by Taylor MacBoyer

Charley and Fern are in Fern's bedroom. Fern is painting. She wears a dress and makeup, which look out of place on her and which she's clearly uncomfortable wearing.

CHARLEY: You're an artist.

FERN: I paint pictures. Sunsets, manatees, sea shells, anything the tourist might want to buy.

CHARLEY: You must be pretty good.

FERN: No.

CHARLEY: People buy them?

FERN: They're pretty horrible. Pretty and horrible.

CHARLEY: But people buy them.

FERN: People don't have good taste.

CHARLEY: I'm sure they're better than you think.

FERN: They're not. My last . . . whatever, he left me because they were chintzy.

CHARLEY: Your boyfriend?

FERN: Whatever.

CHARLEY: He left you cause of your painting?

FERN: If you are what you do and what you do is chintzy . . . I was doing chintzy art and he was doing me, connect the dots.

CHARLEY: Do you get defined by what you do?

FERN: Of course not. So, what do you do Charley?

CHARLEY: You're not chintzy.

(Fern unveils one of her paintings, of two sea cows. It's horribly chintzy.)

FERN: Hugh and Buffet.

CHARLEY: It's . . .

FERN: What I'm capable of.

CHARLEY: They're so-

FERN: So.

CHARLEY: Well . . .

FERN: They're responsible for the mermaid legend.

CHARLEY: Those?

FERN: This is my current project.

(She turns the painting she has been working on over.)

CHARLEY: Oh.

FERN: A red tide bloom. *Gymnodinium breve* to be exact. A modern day Leviathan.

CHARLEY: Pretty-

FERN: Toxic. It has silicone in the cell walls. Like fake breasts.

CHARLEY: You like to paint toxic things?

FERN: Trying something different. It's not working. Pink Fluffy, Cute. That's what little girls like and that's what I do. Only, if you're still sleeping with your stuffed animals when you're thirty . . . it's OK. I don't want to be Van Gogh. What exactly did my father tell you, about me?

CHARLEY: You're pretty infamous in town.

FERN: Great.

CHARLEY: "Guru Girl Takes A Gulp!"

FERN: Thank you.

CHARLEY: Did it hurt?

FERN: Breathing water? Not really.

CHARLEY: Were you disappointed.

FERN: That it didn't work or that it didn't hurt?

CHARLEY: Both.

FERN: Doctor thinks my neurotransmitters are messed up.

CHARLEY: You're..?

FERN: Went to the hospital for the first time since birth. Doctor said I'm delusional and that I could take medication for it.

CHARLEY: So why don't you?

FERN: I'm a Christian Scientist.

CHARLEY: That's so weird.

FERN: Aren't you a Christian Scientist?

CHARLEY: Why would you think that?

FERN: You met my father at church.

CHARLEY: Oh well, I just like to go to church.

FERN: Any church?

CHARLEY: Ones where you have to stand up and talk.

FERN: You like talking?

CHARLEY: No, am I talking too much?

FERN: I just . . .

CHARLEY: No, it's part of my self-help group. We have to do things we're scared of. I'm trying to improve myself. Step three.

FERN: Does my father know you're not a Christian Scientist?

CHARLEY: No, you're not supposed to lie but it's a process. Are you gonna tell him?

FERN: Why are you here?

CHARLEY: He asked me —

FERN: No, why are you here?

CHARLEY: You should come . . . to group.

FERN: Is it helping . . . a group teaching self-help.

CHARLEY: (it's not) Oh yeah.

FERN: What do you do Charley?

CHARLEY: Do?

FERN: For a living?

CHARLEY: I get paid.

FERN: A lot.

CHARLEY: Shit loads.

FERN: Does father know that?

CHARLEY: I think so.

FERN: And that's why you're here?

CHARLEY: You don't remember me huh?

FERN: I'm sorry?

CHARLEY: We went to school together. You don't remember me.

FERN: I'm sorry.

CHARLEY: I sat behind you in . . . doesn't matter.

FERN: A lot's happened since then.

CHARLEY: I know.

FERN: Did we used to talk?

CHARLEY: No, I mean sometimes we'd have to 'cause the teacher would pair us . . .

FERN: Did we ever . . . ?

CHARLEY: No, no, no, no, no, no.

FERN: After a point everyone looks like someone you've slept with.

CHARLEY: We never . . .

FERN: But I was mean to you.

CHARLEY: Never.

FERN: Just didn't pay you any attention.

CHARLEY: You should take medication for that neuro brain thingy you have.

FERN: Not so sure it's me that's got things backwards. Not so sure I want my neurotransmitters working properly. Geometry.

CHARLEY: Right.

FERN: You used to come in all banged up.

CHARLEY: Well,

FERN: All the time. Black and blue.

CHARLEY: Not all the time.

FERN: Not from fighting though.

CHARLEY: Well.

FERN: You're not the type. *(Pause. Fern begins to cry. Charley doesn't know what to do.)* Can I take you somewhere Charley?

CHARLEY: We're not supposed to leave the house.

FERN: Someplace special.

Monologue Edited from
RED TIDE BLOOMING

FERN
any age
seriocomic

I paint pictures. Sunsets, manatees, seashells, anything the tourist might want to buy. They're pretty horrible. Pretty and horrible. People buy them but people don't have good taste. My last . . . whatever, he left me because they were chintzy. If you are what you do and what you do is chintzy . . . I was doing chintzy art and he was doing me, connect the dots. This is my current project. A red tide bloom. *Gymnodinium breve* to be exact. A modern day Leviathan. It has silicone in the cell walls. Like fake breasts. I've been trying something different. It's not working. Pink, fluffy, cute. That's what little girls like and that's what I do. Only, if you're still sleeping with your stuffed animals when you're thirty . . . It's OK, I don't want to be Van Gogh. The doctor thinks my neurotransmitters are messed up. Went to the hospital after my incident and the doctor said I'm delusional, that I could take medication for it. Not so sure it's me that's got things backwards. Not so sure I want my neurotransmitters working properly. Geometry. You sat behind me in Geometry, I remember now. I'm not as pretty as I used to be huh? But still pretty enough right? Let me take you someplace. I want to share something with you. Let me show you something special, yeah?

DISCUSSION OF MONOLOGUE EDITED FROM
RED TIDE BLOOMING

Fern gets to tell Charley all about herself and her life in this character monologue. We get to see the relationship that she's had with him in the past, and the (possibly) future one she may have. By cutting out all of Charlie's reactions to what is being said to him, we end up with a quaint character monologue, useful for auditions where similar characters to Fern are being cast.

• • •

Original Scene from
MURMURS by Scott C. Sickles

Les is eighteen years old, a high school senior who doesn't fit in.

JASON: Are all your friends going away, too?

LES: I suppose. They're not my friends, really. They're acquaintances.

JASON: What's the difference?

LES: Friends . . . at least in my opinion . . . are more than people you eat lunch with five days a week.

JASON: So, are we acquaintances then? You and me?

LES: We're lab partners.

JASON: And baseball enthusiasts.

LES: I don't know if I'd go that far.

JASON: So, you don't have any friends? Just acquaintances?

LES: You probably think that's weird.

JASON: I think I grasp the concept.

LES: You can't rely on anyone. They'll borrow your social studies notes, but won't talk to you when they're with their friends.

JASON: Am I like that?

LES: Not that I've noticed. But, anyway, I hate it. Sometimes I think . . . Did you ever see *Invasion of the Body Snatchers*?

JASON: Uh . . . no. Not all the way through.

LES: You know about the pod people? About how they replace humans with doubles that don't have any personalities?

JASON: Kind of like study hall. Yeah, I know about them.

LES: Well, the way I see it is —

JASON: There's a remake coming out soon, with Donald Sutherland.

LES: Really? Interesting. I'll have to catch it. Anyway, what I was —

JASON: Maybe we can see it together.

LES: Sure. That'd be . . . great. My point was: it seems that even though the pod people are these soul-less robots, at least they're consistent. You know what I mean? They're loyal. In a way, it's like they're devoted to each other.

JASON: Are you saying you want to be a pod person?

LES: No . . . I guess I want humans to get along as well as alien races bent on world domination. Is that so wrong?

Monologue Edited from
MURMURS

LES
eighteen
dramatic

Yeah, all of my friends are going away this summer, too. They're not my friends, really. They're acquaintances. Friends . . . at least in my opinion . . . are more than people you eat lunch with five days a week.

You're a popular guy. You probably think that's weird . . . only having acquaintances. Thing is: you can't rely on anyone. They'll borrow your social studies notes, but won't talk to you when they're with their friends. I don't mean . . . Not you. At least, not that I've noticed. But, anyway, I hate it. Sometimes I think . . . Did you ever see *Invasion of the Body Snatchers*? You know about the pod people? About how they replace humans with doubles that don't have any personalities? Like in study hall? Well, the way I see it is: it seems that even though the pod people are these soul-less robots, at least they're consistent. You know what I mean? They're loyal. In a way, it's like they're devoted to each other. *(Pause. Realizes he's being weird.)* I'm not saying I want to be a pod person. It's just . . . I guess I want humans to get along as well as alien races bent on world domination. Is that so wrong?

DISCUSSION OF MONOLOGUE EDITED FROM *MURMURS*

Once again, we see how turning a two-person scene into a successful audition monologue can be quite simple. The conversation in this particular scene lends itself to monologue material. Finding good scenes in plays that can be adapted in this way is what you'll need to make up original audition monologues such as this.

Appendix B
Recommended Books

Alterman, Glenn. *Creating Your Own Monologue.* Allworth Press, 1999.

———. *Two Minutes and Under.* Lyme, NH: Smith and Kraus, 1993.

———. *Two Minutes and Under,* Vol. 2. Lyme, NH: Smith and Kraus, 2002.

Beard, Jocelyn A., ed. *The Best Men's Stage Monologues of 1998.* Lyme, NH: Smith and Kraus, 1999.

———. *The Best Women's Stage Monologues of 1996.* Lyme, NH: Smith and Kraus, 1997.

———. *One Hundred Men's Stage Monologues from the 1980s.* Lyme, NH: Smith and Kraus, 1991.

———. *The Ultimate Audition Book: 222 Monologues 2 Minutes and Under.* Lyme, NH: Smith and Kraus, 1997.

Davidson, Gordon, ed. *The Great Monologues from the Mark Taper Forum.* Lyme, NH: Smith and Kraus, 1994.

Early, Michael, and Philippa Keil, eds. *Solo: The Best Monologues of the 80s (Men).* Applause Theater Books, 1987.

————. *Solo: The Best Monologues of the 80s (Women)*. Applause Theater Books, 1987.

Emerson, Robert, and Jane Grumbach, eds. *Monologues, Men: 50 Speeches from Contemporary Theater,* vol. 1, vol. 2, vol. 3. New York: Drama Book Publishers, 1976, 1982, 1989.

Friedman, Ginger Howard. *The Perfect Monologue: How to Find and Perform the Monologue That Will Get You the Part*. Limelight Editions, 1990.

Graham, Kristen, ed. *The Great Monologues from the EST Marathon*. Lyme, NH: Smith and Kraus, 1992.

————. *The Great Monologues for the Women's Project and Productions*. Lyme, NH: Smith and Kraus, 1994.

Harrington, Laura, ed. *100 Monologues: An Audition Sourcebook from New Dramatists*. Penguin Books, 1989.

Karshner, Roger, ed. *Neil Simon Monologues*. Dramaline Publications, 1996.

Kohlhaas, Karen. *The Monologue Audition: A Practical Guide for Actors*. Limelight Editions, 2002.

Kraus, Eric, ed. *The Great Monologues from the Humana Festiva*. Lyme, NH: Smith and Kraus, 1991.

————. *Monologues from the Plays of Christopher Durang*. Lyme, NH: Smith and Kraus, 2001.

Marlow, Jean, ed. *Audition Speeches for 6–16 Year Olds*. Routledge Theater Arts Books, 2000.

McCullough, L. E. *Ice Babies in Oz*. Lyme, NH: Smith and Kraus, 1995.

Muir, Kerry, ed. *Childsplay: A Collection of Scenes and Monologues for Children*. Limelight Editions, 2001.

Newell, Douglas, ed. *Shakespeare for One, Men: The Complete Monologues and Audition Pieces*. Heinemann, 2002.

———. *Shakespeare for One, Women: The Complete Monologues and Audition Pieces.* Heinemann, 2002.

Pike, Frank, and Thomas G. Dunne. *Scenes and Monologues from the New American Theater.* New American Library, 1988.

Poggi, Jack. *The Monologue Workshop.* Applause Theater Book Publishers, 1990.

Smith, Marisa, and Amy Schewel, eds. *The Actor's Book of Movie Monologues.* New York: Penguin Books, 1988.

Temchin, Jack, ed. *One on One: The Best Men's Monologues for the Nineties.* Applause Books, 1993.

For an extensive selection of monologue anthologies, go to the Smith and Kraus Web site: www.smithandkraus.com.

Permissions

Grateful acknowledgments are made for permission to reprint excerpts from the following plays.

ANCIENT CONTRACT by Ty Adams. © 2001 by Ty Adams. Permission to reprint given by the author. For permission to perform, contact Ty Adams, 17 Casablanca Lane, Woodstock, NY 12498. E-mail: tyadams@casablancalane.com.

ANNIE MAY by Glenn Alterman. © 2002 by Glenn Alterman. Permission to reproduce given by the author. From *Two Minutes and Under, Volume 2* (Smith and Kraus, Inc.). For permission to perform, contact The Glenn Alterman Studio, 400 West 43rd Street, Suite 7G, New York, NY 10036. Tel: (917) 612-5524; e-mail: glennalt@rcn.com.

BACK COUNTY CRIMES by Lanie Robertson. © 1980 by Lanie Robertson. Permission to reproduce given by the author. For permission to perform, contact Howard Rosenstone at Rosenstone/Wender, 38 East 29th Street, New York, NY 10016. Tel: (212) 795-9445.

FORGETTING FRANKIE by Annie Evans. © 2003 by Annie Evans. Permission to reproduce given by the author. For permission to perform, contact Betsy Helf, William Morris Agency, 1325 Avenue of the Americas, New York, NY 10019. Tel: (212) 903-1561.

I'M BREATHING THE WATER NOW by Bash Halow. © 2003 by Bash Halow. Reprinted by permission of the author. Rights available through the author. E-mail: Bhalow@ yahoo.com.

LADY DAY AT EMERSON's BAR AND GRILL by Lanie Robertson. © 1983, by Samuel French. Permission to reproduce given by the author. For permission to perform, contact Howard Rosenstone at Rosenstone/Wender, 38 East 29th Street, New York, NY 10016. Tel: (212) 795-9445.

MERMAID'S BLOOD by Ty Adams. © 1992 by Ty Adams. Reprinted by permission of the author. For permission to perform, contact Ty Adams, 17 Casablanca Lane, Woodstock, NY 12498. E-mail: tyadams@casablancalane.com.

MERMAIDS ON THE HUDSON by Anastasia Traina. © 2002 by Anastasia Traina. Reprinted by permission of the author. For permission to perform, contact Julianne Housler, New York Office, 15 West 26th Street, New York, NY 10010, www.nyoffice.net.

MURMURS by Scott C. Sickles. © 2002 by the Samuel French. Off-Off Broadway Short Play Festival Plays, vol. 21. Permission to reproduce given by the author. For permission to perform, contact Barbara Hogenson, The Barbara Hogenson Agency, Inc., 165 West End Avenue, Suite19-C, New York, NY 10023.

NASTY LITTLE SECRETS by Lanie Robertson. © 1989 by Samuel French. Permission to reproduce given by the author. For permission to perform, contact Howard Rosenstone, Rosenstone/Wender, 38 East 29th Street, New York, NY 10016. Tel: (212) 795-9445.

NIGHT VISITS by Simon Fill. © 1999 by Simon Fill. Permission to reproduce given by the author. For permission to perform, contact Susan Schulman, A Literary Agency, 454 West 44th Street, New York, NY 10036. Tel: (212) 713-1633.

NOBODY'S FLOOD by Glenn Alterman. © 1998 by Glenn Alterman. Permission to reproduce given by the author. For permission to perform, contact The Glenn Alterman Studio, 400 West 43rd Street, Suite 7G, New York, NY 10036. Tel: (917) 612-5524; e-mail: glennalt@rcn.com.

POST PUNK LIFE by Simon Fill. © 1997 by Simon Fill. Permission to reproduce given by the author. For permission to perform, contact Susan Schulman, A Literary Agency, 454 West 44th Street, New York, NY 10036, (212) 713-1633.

RED TIDE BLOOMING by Taylor MacBowyer. © 2002 by Taylor MacBowyer. Permission to reproduce given by the author. For permission to perform, contact Taylor MacBowyer, 149 West 14th Street, #5, New York, NY 10011.

THE ROOM INSIDE THE ROOM I'M IN by Simon Fill. © 1998 by Simon Fill. Permission to reproduce given by the author. For permission to perform, contact Susan Schulman, A Literary Agency, 454 West 44th Street, New York, NY 10036. Tel: (212) 713-1633.

RUNNING QUARTER HORSES by Mary Sue Price. © 1994 by Mary Sue Price. Permission to reproduce given by the author. For permission to perform, contact Ricki Olshan, Don Buchwald and Associates, 10 East 44th Street, New York, NY 10017. Tel: (212) 867-1200.

SACRED JOURNEY By Matthew Witten. © 1994 by Matthew Witten. Permission to reproduce given by the author. For permission to perform, contact Judy Boals, Berman, Boals and Flynn, 208 West 30th Street, #401, New York, NY 10001. Tel: (212) 868-1068.

SHEPHERD'S BUSH by Scott C. Sickles. © 1999 by Scott C. Sickles. Permission to reproduce given by the author. For permission to perform, contact Barbara Hogenson, The Barbara Hogenson Agency, Inc., 165 West End Avenue, Suite19-C, New York, NY 10023.

SOLACE by Glenn Alterman. © 2001, by Glenn Alterman, Reprinted by permission of the Author. For permission to perform, contact The Glenn Alterman Studio, 400 West 43rd St, #7G, New York, NY 10036.

THE SUN AND THE MOON LIVE IN THE SKY by Ellen Lewis. © 1990 by Ellen Lewis. Reprinted by permission of the author. For permission to perform, contact Barbara Hogenson, The Barbara Hogenson Agency, Inc., 165 West End Avenue, Suite19-C, New York, NY 10023.

TO BUILD A DREAM ON by Joe Pintauro. © by Joe Pintauro. Permission to reproduce given by the author. For permission to perform, contact David Williams, Don Buchwald Agency, 10 E 44 Street, New York, NY, 10017.

UNCLE PHILIP'S COAT by Matty Selman. © 1998 by Matty Selman. Permission to reproduce given by the author. For permission to perform, contact Jane Alderman, Chilany Pictures, 640 N. La Salle Street, #535, Chicago, IL 60610. Tel: (312) 397-1182.

VIRGINS IN ASTORIA By Phil Hines, Phil Hines. © 2001 by Phil Hines. Reprinted by permission of the author. For permission to perform, contact Phil Hines, 35-50 85th Street, 6-H, Jackson Heights, NY 11372. E-mail: Phines2031@ aol.com.

WHITE RIVER by Mary Sue Price. © 1990 by Mary Sue Price. Permission to reproduce given by the author. For permission to perform, contact Ricki Olshan, Don Buchwald and Associates, 10 East 44th Street, New York, NY 10017. Tel: (212) 867-1200).

WILD ECHINACEA by Jonathan Reuning. © 1997 by Jonathan Reuning. Permission to reproduce given by the author. For permission to perform, contact Jonathan Reuning, 47-12 48th Street, #2R, Woodside, NY 11377. E-mail: jonathanreuning@eatheatre.org.